FROM STRAWI FIELDS TO ABBE

A Billy Shears Story

Bob Wilson and Donald Jeffries

BearManor Media.com

Typesetting and layout by BearManor Media

 Published in the USA by
BearManor Media
P.O. Box 71436
Albany, GA 31708
www.BearManorMedia.com

Softcover Edition
ISBN-10:
ISBN-13: 979-8-88771-165-2

Published in the USA by Bear Manor Media

DEDICATED TO THE FAB THREE:

My friends Jude, Johana, and Ivor.

FOREWORD

Jude Southerland Kessler

Author of *The John Lennon Series*

In their book *The Walrus Was Ringo*, noted authors Alan Clayson and Spencer Leigh wryly comment, "A habit of reading hidden meanings in record grooves left the runway when the music of certain pop stars was elevated from ephemera to Holy Writ. This was, of course, during the time that Roy Orbison called 'the crazy late sixties when it got real weird – politics, music, fashion. Everything went crazy, sort of.' A classic example was the man who was so obsessed with analyzing Bob Dylan's lyrics…in order to prove…that [Dylan's] stimulant intake affected his muse [that the researcher] placed a 'wanted' advertisement in a New York underground magazine for a Dylan urine sample!" (p. 234)

Clayson and Leigh go on to say that during this time frame, "Likewise, Beatle fans…began listening to their records in the dark, at the wrong speeds, backwards. Every inch of the sleeves and labels was scrutinized for veiled but oracular messages that would [make] listeners…truly at one with The Beatles." And in this atmosphere, the "Paul is Dead" controversy was born.

The tragic story that Paul McCartney had been killed in a 9 November 1966 car accident and had been summarily replaced by an extremely talented look-alike/sound-alike took root and began to diffuse rapidly through the fan base. Soon, hints and clues and even ironic songs by other groups touting the death of Paul (or making jest of the rumor) sprung up. Evidence abounded on *Sgt. Pepper* and in *Strawberry Fields Forever* and at the end of *I'm So Tired*. In myriad photos and lyrics, the bizarre legend took on a life of its own. But was it true or was this phenomenon the stuff of fandom gone awry?

In the fall of 2021, I was a guest on George Noory's *Coast to Coast* syndicated radio show, and Noory asked me to weigh in on the "Paul is Dead" controversy. Being a lifelong Lennon expert, I stated that I had spent precious little time studying that particular body of evidence, and I really knew nothing about it. When pressed for an opinion, one way or the other, however, I shrugged and said that I found it highly unlikely that The Beatles entourage could have discovered another human being who so closely resembled Paul McCartney and who possessed McCartney's unique ability to write unforgettable songs and to sing them with such utter grace. Over the next few weeks, I received numerous e-mails castigating me for my sheer ignorance and providing me with a wealth of information on the "Paul is Dead" debate. One person threatened bodily harm if I didn't "come to believe." This topic, I discovered, is clearly still of great interest to some fans, and it is backed by very strong opinions.

In that vein, Bob Wilson and Don Jeffries have, in this volume, provided us all with a new look at the mysterious dilemma which emerged almost 60 years ago. They have asked Beatles fans, authors, and associates to comment on the story and to shed new light on this complicated situation. I am looking forward to reading this book along with you and learning more about the thorny and still quite controversial topic. Perhaps now that the dust has settled, Wilson and Jeffries will uncover a nugget of the truth that will set this story aright. And then again, perhaps not. After all, the best mysteries remain mysteries forever, don't they?

Nevertheless, come with me into the pages beyond, if you will. Let's explore this quandary together. To quote Emily Wofford's third grade teacher, "We shall see what we shall see." (Who is Emily Wofford? Another mystery.)

NOTE: The QR Code on the following page comes courtesy of Rande Kessler, who told us: "You simply place this on the book page like you would any photo or picture, etc. To use it to go to the site, the "user" just holds their phone up to the code so that the entire code is in the frames; a small oval shape will appear at the bottom, you just touch that oval and it takes your phone to the site." This takes the reader to Bob Wilson's interview with Bruce Spizer.

INTRODUCTION

Donald Jeffries

We were driving through Colorado, we had the radio on, and eight of the Top 10 songs were Beatles songs..."I Wanna Hold Your Hand," all those early ones. They were doing things nobody was doing. Their chords were outrageous, just outrageous, and their harmonies made it all valid...I knew they were pointing the direction of where music had to go.

—Bob Dylan

The Beatles, consisting of Liverpool natives John Lennon, Paul McCartney, George Harrison, and Ringo Starr, are still the top selling band in the history of popular music. They had the most number one hits, and on April 4, 1964, they accomplished something no one ever had, or ever will again. On that date, they boasted the *top five* singles on Billboard's Hot 100. The following week, they shattered the record for most songs charting at the same time, when fourteen of their songs appeared in the Hot 100. Collectively, they were incomparable, the Babe Ruth of entertainers. I explored the concept of fame in my recent book *On Borrowed Fame: Money, Mysteries, and Corruption in the Entertainment World.* I believe that the Beatles might very well be the most famous people of all time.

Testimonials to their impact are everywhere. George Thorogood declared that their influence was such that "10%" of the earnings from the groups that came after them "should have gone right into their pocket!" Future rock stars from Joe Walsh (who stated he said "f*ck school" after watching them on *The Ed Sullivan Show*) to Tom

Petty (who talked about it looking "like so much fun") began dreaming after seeing the Fab Four for the first time, and it wasn't long before there was a boom in guitar and drum set sales. Ed Sullivan himself remembered "the bedlam that was occasioned by their debut...Broadway was jammed with people for almost eight blocks...There has never been anything like it in show business..." Keith Richards and Mick Jagger were especially grateful to the Beatles, for giving them the Lennon-McCartney composition *I Wanna Be Your Man,* which became the Rolling Stones' first big hit in Great Britain. Alice Cooper said, "Everybody was influenced by the Beatles." Outside the world of music, comedian Jerry Seinfeld spoke for millions of fans when he declared that "Whenever a Beatles song comes on the radio, I reach for the volume and turn it up, because I still haven't gotten enough of them." Even perhaps America's last great novelist, Kurt Vonnegut, noted, "I say in speeches that a plausible mission of artists is to make people appreciate being alive at least a little bit. I am then asked if I know of any artists who pulled that off. I reply, 'The Beatles did.'" George Harrison claimed that "The Beatles saved the world from boredom." A typically strident John Lennon exclaimed, "Don't you think that the Beatles gave every sodden thing they've got to be the Beatles? That took a whole section of our youth - that whole period - when everyone else was just goofin' off we were workin' 24 hours a day!"

Nearing the end of 1966, the Beatles had already accomplished more than any other musical group in recorded history. They'd had countless hit records, with an incredible twelve going to number one on the charts. That number would eventually reach a record twenty. They'd gradually and successfully transitioned from the early contagious pop that created *Beatlemania* into a harder, more diverse and sophisticated sound. They had already invented the music video, which would eventually lead to the advent of MTV in the 1980s. Their 1964 film *A Hard Day's Night* displayed their unique comedic sense, which was compared to the Marx Brothers, and their wholesome charm. It was a smash critical and box office success, and was nominated for two Academy Awards. They sold incredible amounts of merchandise, including Beatles wigs, which I donned as a seven-year-old super fan, in a grade school "band" where we played their second album and sang along to *She Loves You* and the other songs. There was even an animated cartoon series *The Beatles,* which ran from 1965-1967 on ABC's Saturday morning lineup. Their voices weren't used, but their images were so familiar and beloved that it didn't matter to fans.

This book is a bit different from all the others recounting the incredible story of the four Lads from Liverpool. We will cover that, but with an emphasis on a remarkable legend, one that almost certainly couldn't be true. It was probably a fantastic promotional device cooked up by creative manager Brian Epstein, or perhaps simply by the Beatles themselves. The names John, Paul, George, and Ringo had already been etched into the minds of Americans, and were an indispensable part of Baby Boomer culture. So, if one of them had tragically died at the peak of their fame, at such a tender age, obviously that would shock the world.

The legend goes that Paul McCartney, half of the world's most prolific songwriting team along with John Lennon, died in an automobile accident on November 9, 1966. Such a story would seemingly be difficult to cover up, but according to the theory the surviving Beatles, fearing the public couldn't withstand the grief, decided to replace Paul with the winner of a McCartney look-alike contest. Usually referred to as William Campbell, or William Shepherd, *aka* Billy Shears, he looked so identical to McCartney that the public was completely fooled. Even more remarkably, he was a left-handed guitarist, and could sing just like Paul. He also had the ability to compose some pretty memorable songs. Sometimes lost in the discussion over this often mocked theory is the fact that the "replacement" would have taken place precisely at the moment in time where McCartney was clearly taking over as the leader of the Beatles from John Lennon, whose prolific creativity was being detrimentally impacted by drugs. Indeed, by their last few albums, if

Billy Shears had taken the place of Paul, he was writing and singing almost every track, and dominating the business side of the band.

The "Paul is Dead" rumor began circulating on college campuses in the fall of 1969. As a seventh grader who had already purchased a lot of Beatles records, I was entranced as it swept through my own Luther Jackson Intermediate School. One kid in my gym class was already an expert on all the clues one could find on the album covers, or by playing records backwards. I couldn't figure out how to play a record backwards. Fred LaBour, bassist for the band Riders in the Sky, is generally credited with starting the whole phenomenon. While a staff writer for the *Michigan Daily,* LaBour had been assigned the enviable task of reviewing the Beatles new album, *Abbey Road.* On Oct. 12, 1969, LaBour was listening to radio station WKNR from Detroit, and heard disc jockey Russ Gibb take a call from a listener, who wanted to talk about the intriguing new rumor that Paul McCartney was dead. The caller went over some of the clues pointing to McCartney's death, which were supposedly hidden in the Beatles' lyrics, and photographs of the band. Gibb subsequently fielded a number of listener calls on this hot new topic. The following day LaBour would write what *Michigan Today* would call "one of the oddest and most influential record reviews ever printed." A headline across the second page of the *Michigan Daily* proclaimed, "McCartney dead; new evidence brought to light." LaBour's full-page article began, "Paul McCartney was killed in an automobile accident in early November, 1966, after leaving EMI recording studios tired, sad, and dejected." McCartney would later be found, "pinned under his car in a culvert with the top of his head sheared off. He was deader than a doornail." LaBour credited John Lennon with orchestrating the cover-up. LaBour's article took the community by storm, quickly selling out. LaBour recounted hearing Beatles music wherever he walked, including occasional instances where someone was trying to play a record backwards.

The clues that Lennon and the Beatles allegedly left behind included McCartney wearing an arm patch in a photo on the insider cover of *Sgt. Pepper's Lonely Hearts Club Band*, that seems to read OPD—which according to LaBour was an abbreviation for "Officially Pronounced Dead," the British equivalent of DOA. McCartney is the only Beatle with his back turned in a photo on the album's back cover. Much was made of *Abbey Road's album cover, with the Fab Four walking across the street.* McCartney was curiously barefoot, symbolizing perhaps how corpses are buried without shoes. Some have speculated that George Harrison is dressed like a grave digger, while Ringo Starr represents a pallbearer, and John Lennon the preacher. In the photo Paul holds a cigarette in his right hand, whereas he was one of the world's more notable left-handers. His eyes are also curiously closed, unlike the others. In the background a Volkswagen Beetle bears the license plate "LMW 28IF." True believers maintained that this meant McCartney would have been 28 if he were alive. Actually, he would have been 27, but close enough for some. When played backwards, the Beatles song *Revolution 9* supposedly said "Turn me on, dead man." The outro of *I Am the Walrus,* meanwhile, revealed the eerie chorus of "Ha ha! Paul is dead." *Strawberry Fields Forever* supposedly said "I Buried Paul" when played backwards. The song *Come Together* was alleged to refer to Paul speaking himself, as in "over me." John's disclosure that "the walrus was Paul" in the song *Glass Onion,* was an acknowledgment that the walrus is the Indian symbol of death. On the cover of *Sgt. Pepper's,* a hand appears over McCartney's head. This was supposedly an eastern symbol of death. A hand would appear over Paul's head on the cover of the *Yellow Submarine* LP as well. The odd funereal type flower arrangement under the band members on the cover features a left-handed bass guitar, such as the one Paul played, with only three strings on it, representing the surviving Beatles. In the booklet accompanying the album, why is Paul sitting in front of a sign that inexplicably reads, "I You Was?" On another page, he is wearing a black carnation while the other Beatles have red ones. Similarly, in the video for the song *Your Mother Should Know*, off the *Magical Mystery Tour* album, the other

Beatles are wearing red roses, while Paul is sporting a black one. As was pointed out in an otherwise skeptical article, Paul's explanation that they ran out of red roses is contradicted by the fact he's seen being handed a big bouquet of red roses, while he is wearing the black one.

Most of these clues - more than two dozen - came from Fred LaBour's article. LaBour readily admitted that he invented the clues himself as a joke. LaBour was shocked at how much attention the "Paul is Dead" phenomenon garnered almost instantly. "The story was quoted extensively everywhere," LaBour said. "First the Detroit papers, then Chicago, then, by the weekend, both coasts." "Paul is Dead" was seriously covered on all three major network newscasts, and stories appeared in *Time* and *Life* magazines. But if LaBour made the entire thing up, then what was the caller talking about on the radio show, which is said to have been his inspiration? Where did the caller hear the rumor, *before* LaBour's article?

Actually, there are several earlier references to the Paul rumor, predating LaBour. A November 21, 1966 article in the *UK Daily Express* reported, "Beatle fans crowded round the young man at Nairobi Airport nine days ago. But he waved them away saying: 'I'm not Paul McCartney, but I'm sometimes mistaken for him.' But tonight the secret came out after the Beatle Paul - his hair cropped and sporting a moustache - flew back to London from an undisturbed safari holiday. 'We were all sworn to secrecy,' said a travel firm spokesman." Whatever this odd story means, it is noteworthy that it was published so shortly after Paul's supposed death on November 9. *Rolling Stone* magazine would claim that someone had approached them with some "Paul is Dead" clues in the fall of 1968. Illinois University's student newspaper, the *Northern Star*, ran an article on September 23, 1969, headlined "Clues Hint at Possible Beatle Death." Less than a week earlier, on September 17, Tim Harper wrote a story in the college newspaper of Drake University. At the time, Harper achieved some notoriety for being the first to publicize all the clues. On October 23, 1969, the *Des Moines Register* reported that Harper had been paid for several interviews and appeared on a local Chicago morning television show. Harper was quoted in the October 23, 1969 *Chicago Sun-Times* as declaring, "It was just a joke. I was the first one to put it all together. I knew when I wrote the story that it wasn't true." Just like LaBour, Harper seemed to be claiming authorship of the "Paul is Dead" urban legend. Most incredibly, the November 2, 1969 edition of *The New York Times* revealed the astonishing fact that Linda Eastman had wondered aloud to a colleague about how she would have loved to meet Paul, but had heard he had died and been replaced by a double. This was in 1967, two years before Linda would marry Paul. The colleague in question, J. Marks, sent a wedding message to Paul that read, "Congratulations whoever you are!"

Regardless, Beatleologist Andru J. Reeve credited LaBour's story with being "the single most significant factor in the breadth of the rumor's spread." While initially concerned that his joke was getting out of hand, LaBour commented, "But after a few days, the theatrical aspect became clearer to me, and, shy as I was in the face of all the attention, I began to enjoy the ride." LaBour participated in a "mock trial" on the rumor in early November, which became an RKO television special starring famous defense attorney F. Lee Bailey. However, the "Paul is Dead" phenomenon seemed to fizzle out as quickly as it caught fire. The special aired only once, on a local TV station, on November 30, 1969. But the legend lived on, and today there are a surprising number of people who believe that the real Paul McCartney is dead, leaving his replacement with a much longer career than the original Beatle.

Then nineteen-year-old Christine Lahti, a theater student at the University of Michigan in 1969, remembered, "I cannot tell you how many times I listened to those records backwards." Lahti would later become a notable actress, starring in the television series *Chicago Hope*. Skeptical at first, Lahti stated, "After a point you started to hear it, just by the power of suggestion." She pointed out the obvious inference that perhaps all the mind-altering drugs which were popular at the time, might have contributed to the willingness of many young people to accept such dubious information.

On October 21, 1969, the Beatles' press office again issued statements denying the rumor, dismissing it as "a load of old rubbish" and claiming that "the story has been circulating for about two years – we get letters from all sorts of nuts but Paul is still very much with us." Paul McCartney's initial statement regarding the rumor was: "Do I look dead? I am fit as a fiddle. I am alive and well and concerned about the rumors of my death. But if I were dead, I would be the last to know." George Harrison's response in 1969 was to declare, "The rumors are too stupid to bother denying." Ringo Starr declared, "If people are gonna believe it, they're gonna believe it. I can only say it's not true." And John Lennon stated, "It's a lot of nonsense. Paul McCartney couldn't die without the world knowing it. The same as he couldn't get married without the world knowing it. It's impossible-- he can't go on holiday without the world knowing it. It's just insanity. But it's a great plug for *Abbey Road.*" But Lennon seemed to enjoy trolling Beatles fans, as witnessed by the line from his song *Glass Onion*: "Here's another clue for you all - the walrus was Paul." Paul was quoted in *The Beatles: Off the Record* by Keith Badman, as saying, "*I couldn't understand it. First, someone said, 'There's a rumor going around that you're dead.' My first reaction really was just to think, 'Great,' really. Just like James Dean. I just immediately pulled myself back into 15-year-old suburbia, where I saw the James Dean thing enact itself. I was just pleased, you know, because I knew I wasn't dead. So, I just watched the play happen.*" In the November 7, 1969 issue of *Life* magazine, Paul commented, "*Perhaps the rumor started because I haven't been much in the press lately.*" In the *Beatles Anthology* book, published in 2000, Paul noted, "*It was a bit weird meeting people shortly after that, because they'd be looking at the back of my ears, looking a bit through me. And it was weird doing the 'I really AM him' stuff.*" McCartney appeared to be parodying the legend with his 1993 *Paul is Live* LP.

In a 2009 appearance on his late night television show, David Letterman asked Paul about the rumors. McCartney said, "Well, what happened was, we did a cover for a record called *Abbey Road*. And the idea was to walk across the crossing, and I showed up that day with sandals - flip flops. It was so hot that I kicked them off and walked across barefooted. So, this started some rumor that because he was barefooted, he's dead…It was a little bit strange, but people did start looking at me like, is it - is it him, or a very good double?" Some did question the explanation about walking across a road barefoot because it was "too hot." A road would certainly have been a lot hotter on bare feet than with flip flops.

Records satirically or seriously touching on the legend quickly sprung up. There was *The Ballad of Paul* by the Mystery Tour, *Brother Paul* by Billy Shears and the All Americans, *So Long Paul* by Werbley Finster, Zacharias and His Tree People's "We're All Paul Bearers (Parts One and Two) and *Saint Paul* by Terry Knight, which was played on some radio stations in tribute to "the late Paul McCartney." Controversial feminist Camile Paglia ascribed the story to Greek legends of "pretty, long-haired boys," and remarked, "It's no coincidence that it was Paul McCartney, the 'cutest' and most girlish of the Beatles, who inspired a false rumor that swept the world in 1969 that he was dead." National Lampoon's 1972 comedy LP *Radio Dinner* inserted parody clues throughout regarding the legend. The 1978 film spoof *The Rutles: All You Need is Cash* referenced a dead Rutle who'd been replaced, but it was based on the "George" character.

The June 1970 *Batman* comics featured a story in which the Caped Crusader used his incomparable detective skills to investigate what was clearly the "Paul is Dead" theory. For legal reasons, the comic had to change the name of the band to the "Oliver Twists". On the cover, Robin is holding a record album up, on which the story title "Dead Til Proven Alive" is written. Batman says, "One of them is dead - but which one?" On February 23, 1970, a skit on *The Ed Sullivan Show* touched upon the "Paul is Dead" rumor. Two angels in heaven had the following exchange:

Angel One: Is there any truth to the rumor that Paul McCartney is still alive?

Angel Two: I doubt it. Where do you think we get those groovy harp arrangements?

In 2020, a graphic novel was produced, "Paul is Dead: When the Beatles Lost McCartney." One of the comic's creators cryptically explained, "I've never believed in those clues. They're just a bunch of random coincidences discovered by overheated fans. My book is about a strong friendship and four young men coming together and suddenly losing one of their friends…"

Many suspect, as we do, that while Paul never died, the clues may very well have been planted by the Beatles themselves, in what was indeed a brilliant promotional effort. Beatles author and historian Bruce Spizer shared a seemingly explosive confession from Paul McCartney, but it was published on April 1, 2004, and was ultimately just a delicious piece of fiction. Then there is "The Last Testament of George Harrison: Paul McCartney Really is Dead," which contained "newly discovered secret audio tapes." Controversial filmmaker Joel Gilbert released this as part of his 2010 film "Paul McCartney Really is Dead!" In an interview on the Classic Bands web site, Gilbert responded to the obvious problem of some McCartney imposter being able to write all those classic post-1966 songs, by claiming, "Well, in this theory in the film, Lennon says that he and Paul had about fifty songs and ideas that they had already developed that he felt he could pull together and continue The Beatles and continue many McCartney - Lennon compositions even though McCartney was gone." Gilbert even suggests that John Lennon was assassinated just as he was about to publicly expose the hoax. As Gilbert concluded, "there's over a couple hundred clues that Paul McCartney died and they're not coincidental. So, either The Beatles were all in on a massive inside joke to say that Paul McCartney was dead for four or five years during the time of The Beatles, or Paul McCartney really is dead. But the clues are not coincidental. There's too many that are so obviously intentional."

However, a few years after this and other interviews, in which he argued for the Paul is dead theory, Gilbert's website put up the disclaimer, "The 'Paul is Dead' urban legend that exploded worldwide in 1969 was considered a hoax. In this mockumentary spoof of 'Paul-Is-Dead,' a voice on mysterious tapes reveals a secret Beatles history, chronicling McCartney's fatal accident. . . ." In fact, it went from being labeled a "documentary" on the website to "mockumentary" in 2012.

In 2015, a hoax within a hoax quoted Ringo Starr at length, admitting that the real Paul died, and the panicked survivors replaced him with duplicate Billy Shears. It was published on a satirical web site, but still many believed it. Billy Shears, the most common suspect as "Faul," or the fake Paul McCartney, produced the inevitable book, *The Memoirs of Billy Shears,* in 2009. Surprisingly, the book featured a Foreword from Gregory Paul Martin, the son of George Martin, legendary producer who has been called the "Fifth Beatle." He also narrated the audio version of the book. This certainly seemed to be an endorsement from him of the legend. The fact that the line, "So let me introduce to you the one and only Billy Shears and Sgt. Pepper's Lonely Hearts Club Band" is an actual lyric on the title track to *Sgt. Pepper's,* added to the speculation. True believers maintain that during his 1980 arrest for marijuana possession in Tokyo, fingerprints taken from the alleged former Beatle did not match the historical McCartney's, although others claim there is no evidence for this. Still, public belief in the conspiracy theory appears to be diminishing. A 2013 poll found only five percent of respondents believed Paul died in 1966.

There are lots of people out there, in the alternative media, who seriously believe that Paul McCartney died in 1966, and was replaced by a very talented duplicate. An analysis by two forensic research consultants was published in 2009 by *Wired Italia* magazine. They compared selected photographs of McCartney taken before and after his alleged death by measuring features of the skull. The researchers concluded that the individual in the post-November

1966 images was not the same as the original Beatle. "Paul is Dead" true believers claim that the current Paul's DNA was proven in a German court (why Germany?) to be different from the historical Paul McCartney's. A professor in Florida claims the voiceprints from Paul and "Faul" are different. In 2009, *Time* magazine named the "Paul is Dead" rumor as one of "the world's most enduring conspiracy theories." Peter Blake, who designed the cover of the iconic *Sgt. Pepper's Lonely Hearts Club Band* album, would relate, *"I was with Paul on the day that the rumour broke and he said to me, 'Yes, it's true. I'm not actually Paul McCartney. You know Paul McCartney, he didn't have a scar on his mouth. I'm very like him, but I'm actually not him.' I looked, and indeed there was a scar, but Paul didn't have a scar. What had happened was that he had fallen off his bike (1966) and had got a scar since I last saw him [sic]. Of course, it was Paul, and he did kid me for two minutes. And for three minutes I did believe him."*

So despite the implausibility of the thing, we decided that the subject was worthy of a book. We reached out to many celebrities, music industry insiders, and Beatles researchers, to get their input on what the Beatles meant to them, and in particular their thoughts on the whole "Paul is Dead" phenomenon. We have published the questions we asked them, and their responses, with only minimal editing for punctuation.

This book is Bob Wilson's baby. It was his idea. He contacted most of the people, and asked the questions. I helped where I could. It was a labor of love for both of us. The Beatles continue to fascinate, to such an extent that even a legend that, on the surface, seems preposterous resonates with people all over the world. Could it possibly have happened? Did the Beatles knowingly set up the hoax, leaving tantalizing clues within their work? You decide. It's been nearly sixty years since they burst upon the scene, but the four Lads from Liverpool have proven to have truly lasting staying power.

A NOTE FROM BOB WILSON

This book puts the focus on the memories of noteworthy people, who have a love of the Beatles in common. Many of these people have been guests on the *Tomorrow Never Knows* podcast, or been interviewed by me in various articles. They came together to help tell this story from their own unique viewpoints. We do not really question if Paul Lives, but recount how these clues caused a reaction throughout the world that touched the lives of so very many people.

As much as the Beatles have meant to me, there is something that is even more special. Getting to interact and know the people we interviewed has provided the real enjoyment for me. They have shared their time and stories, and their company has been even better (dare I say it?), than spinning a Beatles disc. There are not too many things that are in that category.

Don Jeffries is a noted author and friend. Don accepted when I asked him to be my co-author on this one. His insight and professionalism put my mind at ease, and made the proceedings all the more entertaining. Warren Brown can say in a picture what we can't say in ten thousand words. You can see that clearly on the front and back covers of this work. Sir Warren has become a beloved fixture among Beatle fans, and a brother in my heart.

Dear sir or madam, thank you for having a look. There are places I remember in sharing the Beatles with all of you, and you have allowed us to present the noteworthy people who expound on their memories found herein. There have been many discussions on who the fifth Beatle is. I realized tonight that the collective fifth Beatle are the fans.

DEDICATED TO THE FAB THREE: My friends Jude, Johana, and Ivor.

PROMINENT RECOLLECTIONS

Fred LaBour

Fred LaBour, as indicated in the Introduction, is often credited with inventing the "Paul is Dead" legend. He is an accomplished musician himself whose band has won two Grammys.

Please tell us about yourself, your band, your Grammys, and what you have cooking in the works now, Too Slim?

I'm Fred LaBour. I graduated from the University of Michigan in 1971 with an associate degree in wildlife management. I bought a bass guitar in the autumn of that year and taught myself to play. I worked in several bands including a successful country band where I got the notion to write country songs. I wrote and demoed some tunes along with my band mates, and took them to Nashville where they attracted some interest. I moved here in October of 1972 and happened to move in next door to Ranger Doug who, like me, was a lifelong Detroit Tigers fan. We played together in various ensembles—bluegrass, swing, and country—until he got the idea to form a band and just play western music in the tradition of the Sons of the Pioneers, Roy Rogers, and Gene Autry. We played our first gig as Riders in the Sky on Nov. 11, 1977. Since then we've played, as of last night, 7716 shows, traveled over five million miles to every state in the USA plus 13 countries, made 40 albums, won two Grammys for our *Woody's Roundup* and *Monsters, Inc.* albums, created and starred on TV for CBS and TNN, etc. created 250 public radio shows, and just celebrated our 40th anniversary as members of the Grand Ole Opry where we regularly appear when we're not on the road. My songwriter highlight is that I'm the only person on the planet, the only person in history, who can say "I've had my songs recorded by Tammy Wynette, William Shatner, and…wait for it… Don Rickles."

It's 1969, and you are a UM - natural resources student with a very devious and creative mind. When did the idea light bulb go off, and strike you with the notion that Paul McCartney had been replaced in the Beatles?

Abbey Road had just come out, and the arts editor at the *Michigan Daily* where I was associate arts editor under Leslie Wayne and my great friend John Gray had assigned the review to me. I was wondering how to approach the review. I happened to be driving from Ann Arbor to Jackson, Michigan on a Sunday afternoon in early October 1969 listening to Russ Gibbs' radio show. I didn't hear the initial call alerting Russ that "something was wrong" with Paul, but I heard Russ' reaction which he kept up for the rest of his show. I think the guy had pointed out the black carnation on the album cover, the hand over Paul's head on *Sgt. Pepper*, and most interestingly the fade out on *Strawberry Fields* which seemed to include a voice saying "I buried Paul." I was fascinated and the hair rose on the back of my neck.

That evening, when I returned to Ann Arbor, I went to my job as Ticket Fred, a ticket taker at Cinema Guild, the campus home of classic and avant garde movies. My friend Jay Cassidy was projectionist and when the movie began he came down from the booth to yak and I told him about the phone call. We laughed about it, made jokes and speculated along the line of "Suppose it's true…" When I got home that night I thought "Okay, that's my review." Next morning I lined up my Beatles albums across the back of my desk and concocted a satirical, and I thought humorous, semi-news story which broke the "news" that Paul had been killed and the Beatles had subsequently released this information to the world through "clues" on album covers and in their music.

Gray was night editor of the arts page, page two in The *Daily*, so I took my story to him that afternoon after class. He laughed so hard, and said "LaBour, you've scooped the world." We laid out the page together, he created the headline. When Leslie stopped by later that night to see what was going on John said, "Don't worry, Leslie. We've got it covered." And she looked at us quizzically and said, "What are you guys up to?" We assured her she'd know in the morning.

Boom, next morning it exploded. The *Daily* sold out and ran an entire extra press run, which I think was unprecedented. In the days to come the story went first to Detroit, then Chicago, then New York, then the west coast, finally to Scotland, where a giant of 20th century music was subjected to the question "Are you alive?"

Devin McKinney credits you as being the mastermind. Will you please tell us about Devin?

I don't know Devin.

As a Grammy Award winning bassist yourself, is that what made you choose Paul to meet his Maker?

It had nothing to do with it because I wasn't playing bass at that time. It had to do with the guy's phone call to Russ Gibb. As a bass player, it's hard to overstate the importance and genius of Paul's work. There is bass playing before Paul, and bass playing after Paul, and you hear his influence literally everywhere in every genre of music. Add in his songwriting, singing, piano, drums, guitar, arranging and you have what can only be described as genius level talent and an unparalleled drive to work, record, and perform.

Which clues can be attributed to your having spotted them? Some seem like a stretch, but other ones seem to have been intentionally placed (such as Turn Me On Dead Man*).*

I didn't know about the *Turn Me On Dead Man* until later. A lot of "clues" came up later and I had nothing to do with them. The ones in the story were all mine, and you're right, the "stretch" you refer to was my letting the reader know that this was a ridiculous piece of satire and not an actual news story. My personal favorite is "Walrus is Greek for corpse." I have a recording of a DJ asking a renowned Greek scholar from Columbia University if walrus is Greek for corpse. To which the professor said "Walroos? What means this walroos?" And still, people believed it. And still, some do to this day!

John Lennon starting a new religion sounds pretty bizarre to the average bear. Can you please clue us in on this aspect of the 'clues'?

Again, part of the satirical overreach. I was burned out on my upper level English courses and I wanted to make fun of the academic predilection for finding "meaning" and "artistic intention" in a work of art. My "meaning" was establishment of a new religion. How ridiculous is that when you're talking about four musicians and a stellar producer and engineer making a pop record?

As all of this was transpiring with you in the nexus, were you becoming well known, and receiving attention?

Yep, I had my 15 minutes of fame, which I've managed to stretch into 17. (Cue laugh) At first I was scared that I'd created this whirlwind of publicity and practically nobody seemed to get the joke. I answered the phone with "It's all true, I made it all up…" for awhile, and then I quit answering the phone altogether. The height of the madness was the F. Lee Bailey mock courtroom TV special which aired around Thanksgiving that year. They flew me and Russ to L.A. and I met Bailey the morning of the show. He quizzed me about all the "clues" and I finally said "You know, I made all this up." There was a marvelous beat of silence, and he said "Well, we have an hour of television to do. You're going to have to play along." To which I said 'OK."

The Beatles stopped touring after Candlestick Park, in San Francisco. Not touring certainly seemed to fit in with the myth of Paul's replacement. What thoughts come to your mind regarding all of that?

Yes, they became an exclusively recording act, and thank God too, because it resulted in *Rubber Soul, Revolver, Pepper*, the *White* album, and *Abbey Road,* each one an absolute classic and genre defining work. Part of my thought process in leading up to the writing was that Ringo had missed some touring in "65, I think. So the notion of a "replacement Beatle" was somehow in the air, or at least in my brain.

Did you ever imagine that in 2022 that your story would still be resonating today? What has led to the longevity?

Never imagined it, never could. I have spent a little time speculating on my role in the creation of today's conspiracy theory madness which the Internet magnifies and uses to divide people and profit from it. I'm not happy about that. The longevity of the rumor probably relates to Paul being a viable monster act to this day, still in the public eye and generating news and selling a whole shitload of tickets.

Did you ever come across any of the Beatles at any point? What do you surmise that they think of your creativity in bringing about this whole chapter in their history?

I've never met a Beatle, regretfully. I saw John in 1971 in Ann Arbor and Paul here in Nashville a couple years ago. I've always thought I should get a fruit basket or something from Paul and Apple thanking me for helping sell millions of records to kids who played them backwards. I've seen interviews with Paul where he clearly gets the joke and the humor of the rumor, so to speak. If I've somehow tormented the life of this incredible artist I'm sorry, but again, that was never my motive.

What would you do if Sir Paul turned around, and started a Fred is Dead rumor? Could you put 'clues' on your album covers, with any backward messages?

I would think it's richly deserved. We've talked a few times in Riders in the Sky about putting a few "clues" on albums or in songs, usually really late at night in the bus rolling down the highway. Never got more serious than that.

So, is Paul still with us? Where do you cast your vote?

Of course he's with us, praise God! I've always dreaded the day when he finally checks out, if indeed it's before I check out, when some yo-yo calls me for a quote about whether or not he's really dead this time. I'll be crying too hard to answer.

Susan Olsen

Susan Olsen starred on the perpetually rerun television show *The Brady Bunch,* playing Cindy, the "youngest one in curls." She has worked as a talk show host, and is presently a fine artist and teaches filmmaking and acting.

Please tell us about yourself, and your work.

I'm best known for playing the youngest member of the Brady Bunch, Cindy. I was a working actress when my age was in the single digits so my view of entertainment is …unique. My first goal in life was to be a Beatle.

When did you first see the Beatles, and how long did it take for you to be hooked?

I remember seeing the Beatles on *Ed Sullivan.* I'm not sure if I saw all three performances because they were all in the same month, February 1964. I was three years old and remember it well. Our cousins were over and the "big girls", who were older than me and wouldn't let me play Barbies with them, were acting crazy. They were squealing and screaming. The teenagers in the televised audience were doing the same. I thought these guys had magical powers. Just look at the power they held over the young ladies, making them cry. I was also half-witted enough to think that they were inside the TV set. Of course, we must have seen all three appearances and I was each time amazed at how my sister would lose her mind and scream while Dad told her to "simmer down." She was only eight but wielded the power in our shared bedroom. By the time I was four and the Beatles had returned to America and our living room, I knew I had to have them. Since they fit inside the TV set, they must be around the size of Barbies and if I could capture them, the big girls would let me play Barbies with them. Makes sense, right? I remember having a plan to keep them in the bathroom sink. It was deep and the sides were steep. They would never be able to scale the walls and escape. Also, should they get messy, they could easily be rinsed.

Which Beatle is your favorite, and what about them makes them stand out?

Of course as a child, my favorite was Paul. He was every girl's favorite. He was the cute one. I found Ringo delightful in *Hard Day's Night.* He was the underdog and I loved him for it. John scared me when I was little. He seemed to be the controversial one and in my eyes he became ugly when he grew his hair and his nose. But they say we are all Johns or Pauls and in my adulthood, I am most definitely a John. I didn't appreciate George until I was old enough to get into Eastern philosophy but that's how it is, my stages of life marked by which Beatle I identified with. They have always been with me. They raised me. By the way, they were never love interests. Reading Ann and Nancy Wilson's book (*Kicking & Dreaming*), they expressed the same thing. It wasn't about dating or marrying a Beatle, it was about BEING a Beatle. God bless them, they did it!

Did you have any experiences where your path crossed with any of the Beatles, or in their solo years?

I'm sad to say that I never met a Beatle. Never even came close! I rode in an elevator with Jimmy Page and Robert Plant when I was a kid and had no idea they would become my rock Gods – but no Beatles. There's still time and still two left…

You have worked with Davy Jones, and he looked quite a bit like Paul. What can you tell us about meeting him?

I didn't think he looked like Paul but he was definitely the cute one! Another year passed and my sister and our nieces were screaming around the television but this time it was a new set of four young men – The Monkees! These guys had a TV show – and it was really funny! I put aside my quest for capturing the Beatles and became a Monkees fanatic. I was in Kindergarten now and terribly hip. I even had a boyfriend; he was the only boy in school with long hair. He knew all the lyrics to every Monkees song. Davy was so cute, all the girls loved him. A new Mexican restaurant had opened in our neighborhood and we loved it. We went at least once a week, maybe more. I remember a bus boy who looked a lot like Davy and a little like Peter. With his limited English, I'm sure he failed to understand what a great compliment I was giving him by telling him that he looked like a Monkee. It also didn't pass my notice that this "cute one" was also from England. England was now the coolest place on Earth. Funny that all of my favorite bands are British. Somehow Americans just didn't have that magick and mystery or butles in their hedgerows. Until grunge, I was never much of a fan of American rock. Later, when Davy appeared on *The Brady Bunch* he was a bit reclusive. My understanding was that he was going through a breakup and not a happy camper. As an adult, I would encounter him several times and he was always the sweetest guy you could ever meet. He was just lovely! Made me feel a bit guilty for the about-face I did in first grade when I decided that I hated the Monkees. Somehow in my warped brain, I felt that I had forsaken

also written many books, including *Hit List* and *UFOs, JFK, and Elvis*.

Will you tell us a bit about yourself, and your work?

I've had a long career as a successful stand-up comic, then an actor – many know me as the long-standing character, Sgt, Munch, on NBC's *Law & Order*. And I'm the author of many books, five of them with my good friend and colleague, David Wayne. I live in France now and I'm very happy here with my wife, Harlee, a former actor herself, and our family of dogs. Looking back, I'm also proud of the documentary I did on *Belzer Connection* about the highly suspicious circumstances surrounding the death of Princess Diana. It was the first really serious look into her death and it was groundbreaking, in that respect. Then I also did a book with David Wayne on the same subject, called *Dead Wrong 2*. But I think I'm proudest of our most recent book, *Corporate Conspiracies: How Wall Street Took Over Washington*, because it ties it all together and shows how our democracy – our Republic – has been co-opted by corporate power and turned into an oligarchy controlled by the 1/10 of 1%, instead of the great experiment in freedom that our forebears so hopefully intended it to be.

Did any of the conspiracies you have researched shock you, as they turned out to be true?

First, since I'm often accused in mainstream media of being an evil conspiracy theorist, I'd like to point out the fact that we don't always arrive at that conclusion. In our book, *Hit List*, for example, there's a table at the back of the book called "Investigatory Results of Fifty Deaths Related to the JFK Assassination" where we conclude that many of those were not directly related to the JFK assassination. But we proved that others were.

Further on that note, as we pointed out in *Corporate Conspiracies*, the phrase "conspiracy theorist" was actually invented by the CIA as a weaponized term to be used to marginalize critics of the official government version of the JFK assassination. That's a documented fact. And they're still doing that today. Plus, they have the blatant cooperation of mainstream media. As an example, *The New York Times* has flatly refused to review any of our books, even though they were on their very own *New York Times Bestseller List!*

So, to answer that question, they *all* shocked me! I find the realities of our world very shocking.

When did you become aware of the Beatles, and how long did it take for you to become a fan?

Immediately, like much of the world. It was like a fever that spread like wildfire. Watching them for the first time on *The Ed Sullivan Show* was like the first worldwide phenomenon. They made an incredible impact on our culture and did so with a tour de force like nothing before them.

Did you have a favorite Beatle, and why are they your favorite?

I would have to say John, due to his courageous political views, especially in the context of the times, as well as his broad world view about human beings learning to live together in peace.

The 1960's really saw things stirred up, and people began to question things. Do you think that atmosphere led to the rumors about Paul's demise?

I think people just like a good story and have a natural tendency to, as you put it, stir things up. Like the old Expression goes; "Don't let the facts get in the way of a good story." And I think it's common nature to do that, but I also think it's necessary to look at things like a detective; to step back and think; "Okay, what here is assumption and what are the actual facts?" But, I also believe that it's extremely important to keep one's mind open to all the possibilities and to always ask, *"Cui bono? Who benefits?"*

On a side note: Bob Dylan also had rumors about his motorcycle accident, and some say that didn't happen. What are your thoughts about Bob Dylan in general, and his accident?

I never really researched his accident, but Dylan was one of the biggest icons of the Sixties, for sure – and deservedly so. His songs were brilliant.

Which of the clues about Paul jump out at you?

I remember thinking that the only ones that even seemed noteworthy were on the albums. On the back of *Sgt, Pepper*, Paul had his back turned while the others faced forward. On *Abbey Road*, Paul was the only one who was barefoot. But proving what? Nothing, really. That's why one has to be careful about researching conspiracies. There truly are many conspiracies – that's a well-proven fact. But, on the other hand, some people reach too far to try and make meaningful connections out of ordinary coincidences. I remember one going around at the time about the similarities between JFK and Abraham Lincoln; that they were both assassinated by Southerners and both succeeded by Southerners who were named Johnson; they were both shot in the head while seated next to their wife; both of their assassins were assassinated before their trials. But, again, proving what? Nothing, positively, except maybe that history repeats itself.

Did you ever play your records backwards?

Nope.

Paul offered to do a soundtrack for Mark Lane's film, Rush To Judgment. *What do you make of that, and Mark Lane's work?*

Mark Lane did some excellent work, very early on, when people were still in shock over the JFK assassination – and then, shortly afterward, the televised assassination of the never-proven-guilty, Oswald, while in police custody. Oswald was actually a member of U.S. Military Intelligence, as we documented in *Dead Wrong*.

But, to me, that just says that Paul McCartney was one of the literally millions of people who saw that there was clearly a difference between what we were officially being told about the JFK assassination and what actually happened. Or, as I put it in my stand-up act: "90 percent of the American people believe that JFK was killed by a conspiracy. The other 10 percent work for the government or the media." That got a lot of laughs, because people innately realized that it was true!

So, is Paul still with us? Where do you cast your vote?
    Yes.

Ivor Davis

Ivor Davis is a veteran British journalist who covered the Beatles on their landmark first American tour. Ivor slept in the same hotels, ate with the Lads from Liverpool, and had the time of his life. Later, Ivor would be in the Ambassador Hotel, covering the Democratic California Primary, on the night Robert F. Kennedy was shot. He also covered the Manson murders and wrote the book *Manson Exposed: A Reporter's 50 Year Journey into Madness and Murder.* His book *The Beatles and Me on Tour* documents his experiences with the Fab Four.

Please give us your bio and highlights of your prestigious work, will you please?
    Ivor Davis was born in London. By pure happenstance he abandoned his parents (before they abandoned him) and took his first ever airplane ride to America. He landed in New York, decided to hitch a ride on a wagon train going west—but none were available. So he took the train to Union Station Los Angeles. By pure luck he became the bureau chief of the *London Daily Express* covering major news stories like Marlon Brando and Cary Grant's divorces. One day they sent him to San Francisco to join a motley band of singers from Liverpool named the Beatles.

How did you get the call to go on tour with the Beatles on their 1964 American tour?

The Foreign Editor of my London newspaper called and ordered me to join the Boys on their first American tour. I wondered what Boys he was referring to. They turned out to be rivals to the Dave Clark Five and the Rolling Stones. So I reluctantly joined them believing I would be touring with Cilla Black. She didn't show up.

I understand John Lennon forced everyone to play Monopoly on the road. Did he ever let you win?

John Lennon might have had a knack for writing songs and singing them—but he was a terrible cheat at Monopoly. He also lost $4 dollars to me at poker—and never paid his debts. To this very day I have tried to contact Yoko Ono to pay up—but she ignores my phone calls.

Is it true that George Harrison did not speak two words on the entire tour? Was he a regular Harpo Marx?

That is a terrible exaggeration. George actually spoke 11 words one day. And by the time the tour ended he had doubled his vocabulary.

We are covering the Paul is Dead rumors. Is it true that Ringo drunkenly said to you in a limo, "Well, John had to write twice as many songs after Paul's demise?"

Not quite: Ringo said something along the lines of, "Paul is definitely not dead—he just danced with that blonde beauty queen that I really fancied. He can't be dead." I interviewed Paul when he was married to Linda—and I can attest it was the same geezer I had traveled with across North America in the year 1964. We had drinks at the Beverly Hills Hotel when he came to Hollywood hoping to win an Oscar for his composition of the Bond movie theme song, *Live and Let Die.*

I interviewed him again about a documentary he was involved in following the drama of 9/11 and Paul was circling Kennedy Airport hoping to land. I grilled him mercilessly about this topic and I can report with utter veracity and certainty that MI5 (Britain's equivalent to the CIA) was not involved in any conspiracy to bump Paul off. I checked with HRH Queen Elizabeth II, who knighted Paul at Buckingham Palace in 1997, and she swears (the Her Majesty doesn't actually swear but you get the picture) that this Paul is the real original Paul. And there is no truth to rumors such as: Vladimir Putin put out a hit on Paul because he didn't like the lyrics to *Back in the U.S.S.R.*

Did you ever play any of your vinyl records backwards?

I was so poor I grew up in a large cardboard box and we never had money to buy a record player. When I became rich and purchased a record player I never mastered the art of playing vinyl backwards.

Is it true that there is an alternate Abbey Road *cover shot by Harry Benson? And in that photo, you were fifth in line in the middle of the lads in the crosswalk? In any way, was the alternate cover a sign?*

Disguised as a parking warden I once chased the Beatles across a zebra crossing but they refused the citation (crossing against a red light) and alas, I didn't have my cell phone camera with me at the time to capture that historic moment.

On the cover of your book Ladies and Gentleman...The Penguins!, *the left-handed bass playing penguin is being poked by the fin of the female lead singing penguin in the eye. In Argentina, penguin flippers are the last meal eaten by death row prisoners. Was this merely a coincidence?*

How clever of you to spot the "leftie" bass player. In Argentina the local penguins prefer eating fried kippers for breakfast. And death row prisoners always go for sardines on toast washed down with a nice Chianti.

Do you think the lads had some fun with these rumors, and some of the clues may have been on purpose?

The lads always had fun and probably came up with the "Paul is Dead" gimmick while heavily inebriated after a night of gargling with rum and coke. Or they thought they needed some original PR idea to help peddle their *Sgt. Pepper* album.

So, is Paul still with us? Where do you cast your vote? :)

I believe Paul is definitely with us. He is now a "HO"—which stands for "Honorable Octogenarian" -- and when last I confronted him backstage at the Petco Stadium in San Diego in the 21st century, he looked very much alive as he wanted to hold the hand of his wife Nancy. Then finally I asked him the Big Question. He calmly turned to me, and with a slight smile noted: "Reports of my death have been greatly exaggerated."

Paul is Dead? No he isn't…he's just resting" (with apologies to *Monty Python's Flying Circus*.) Or maybe he's running a sheep farm in the wilds of Scotland where they don't even have wi-fi. Or maybe one of the most famous octogenarians in the world is high-tailing around Martha's Vineyard with his wife—a lovely lady—and if truth were really told *that* Paul is really a doppelganger. Or maybe there are still some out there—still lost in Beatles Wonderland–who still believe that the man cavorting in front of a sold out Los Angeles Sofi Stadium—or at Britain's Glastonbury Festival in the Summer of 2022—was a fake Paul.

Nick Mancuso

Nick Mancuso is a veteran actor whose career began in 1974, and resulted in over 150 screen credits. He has appeared in many well-known films, but is probably best remembered as the star of the cult 1980s television series *Stingray.* Nick is an iconoclast, and provided a predictably insightful statement to us, without adhering to the question and answer format.

Good to hear from you and yes indeed the Beatles had a massive influence on me and my generation. They in many ways kicked open the doors of the 60s and in that sense the doors of perception Aldous Huxley wrote about in his book. It was all about love with *She Loves You* ya ya ya to John Lennon's *Give Peace a Chance*! If only we could and if only we had listened. The prince of peace and love was of course taken down by an assassin's bullet as was Christ. The oldest story on earth sadly.

Cancer took George Harrison and only Ringo and Paul survived. Ringo was the happy Joker of the group and Paul was the *puer aeternus*, the eternal child who somehow missed the tragedies of life and in many ways continues to send out the beacon of eternal light and hope.

The Beatles represented and still represent eternal optimism. Somehow it was fitting that Paul be declared dead and replaced by a copy because by '69 the souring of the 60s had begun as Freemont and Altamont, Kent State, the war in Vietnam and Charles Manson and the sudden deaths of Jim Morrison, Janis Joplin, Jimi Hendrix destroyed that dream. And the nightmare had begun. Yes Paul was killed in an auto accident as Bob Dylan almost was at Woodstock the very place that had spawned the dream. How ironic.

I never met the Beatles. I've met some of the rock legends - Mick Jagger, Rod Stewart, David Bowie, and performed on stage playing a rock star along with Billy Preston and Mary Clayton in a script co-written by Mick Jagger. I also had the honor of working with the great Leonard Cohen in a film he wrote. But I would very much liked to have known John. To me John was King Arthur and Paul was the lover Sir Lancelot. Yes Camelot briefly returned when the Beatles played. A friend of mine knows Ringo back in Hollywood who gave him some very sound advice. Be happy. Yes indeed. Be Happy. Paul is indeed the Walrus. John is still with us and yes: She does love you. Ya ya ya.

This issue with "the double" or the copy has ancient esoteric roots and has its roots in concepts of immortality in alchemical terms. But there is also a dark side reflecting the issue of the evil twin and the doppelganger. It seems to have particular relevance nowadays where identity is being vacuumed up and revealed open into this brave new world that such creatures in it. Paul's identity theft was the beginning of the spell that finally destroyed it. Merlin made it all happen but the wicked witch of the west took control. Make of that what you will. As John said.

We are all now the walrus. Kooo kooo koooo shoooo.

Fred Velez

Fred Velez is an author and recognized as the foremost expert on The Monkees. He is very knowledgeable about the Beatles as well, and pop culture in general.

Please tell us about yourself, and your work.

I'm Fred Velez, the author of the books *A Little Bit Me, A Little Bit You: The Monkees From A Fan's Perspective* and *A Little Bit Me, A Little Bit You 2: The Monkees From International Fan Perspectives,* both books deal with Monkees fandom from around the world. I'm a long time Monkees and Beatles fan and considered a Pop Culture expert on the history of The Monkees.

You are well versed in the world of the Monkees. How did the Monkees come about, and how did the Monkees and Beatles feel about one another?

The Monkees came about directly from the success of The Beatles when producers Bob Rafelson and Bert Schneider created a television series based on The Beatles. The Beatles were fans of The Monkees TV show and both groups became lifelong friends. Michael Nesmith and his wife Phyliss were weekend guests of John Lennon. Peter Tork played banjo for George Harrison's *Wonderwall'* soundtrack. Micky Dolenz used to hang out with John Lennon, Ringo Starr, Keith Moon and Harry Nilsson and was part of the

Hollywood Vampires in the 1970's. Micky, Davy and Peter also made a surprise appearance in Ringo's humorous Pizza Hut commercial in a send-up of the Beatles reunion rumors.

When did you become aware of the Beatles, and how long did it take for you to be hooked?

Like everyone else I got hooked on The Beatles after their American television debut on the February 9th 1964 *Ed Sullivan Show*. Ironically, future Monkee Davy Jones was on the same show as part of the cast of the Broadway musical *Oliver* in his Tony nominated role of the Artful Dodger. After seeing The Beatles, Davy wanted to get in on that action, too! I followed the Beatles and bought their records and was a fan of the Saturday morning Beatles cartoons.

Who is your favorite Beatle, and why?

I'm a fan of all four Beatles, but I would say that my favorite is Paul McCartney. I loved his work with the Beatles and his solo material too. I've seen Paul in concert many times and I've met and got his autograph along with his late wife Linda. I've also seen Ringo Starr in concert over the years and got to meet him, too. George Harrison was the first Beatle I saw in concert in 1974, and I met John Lennon twice in front of his Dakota apartment in the late 1970's.

Do you recall when you first heard about the Paul is dead rumors?

It was late in 1969 when I first heard the rumors and saw the 'Paul McCartney Dead?' magazine that pointed out the clues. I didn't know what to think at first and checked out the supposed clues that pointed to his death. While it was fascinating at first, I concluded that it was all hearsay and that Paul McCartney was still with us. One of the interesting artifacts of that period was an issue of the *Batman* comic book which dealt with the rumors. I also saw the F. Lee Bailey television report examining the 'Paul is Dead' rumors, where the conclusion was left to the discretion of the viewers.

Which clues stand out in your mind?

Playing '*Revolution 9*' from the *White Album* and hearing "*Turn Me On Deadman*", John Lennon supposedly mumbling during the outro of *Strawberry Fields Forever*, "I Buried Paul" (he actually said "Cranberry Sauce" which is clearly heard on the Beatles Anthology), and clues on some of the Beatles albums that were said to point out that Paul had died.

Did you ever play your vinyl records backwards?

Yes, I played *Revolution 9* backwards to hear the *Turn Me On Deadman* bit; probably ruined my record that way!

Some say that the Beatles stopped touring because Paul was gone. Why do you think the Beatles stopped touring?

By the end of 1966, The Beatles just got fed up with the fans screaming throughout the concerts and not listening, which frustrated them. They were also getting tired of touring, especially after the Philippines and 'Beatles Bigger Than Jesus' fiascos. They'd rather be creating music in the studio and made the decision that the 1966 tour would be their last.

Did the Monkees have any sort of rumors, or any mysteries?

The Monkees didn't have rumors per say. There the controversy that they didn't play the instruments on their records and used studio musicians. They were unfairly singled out since the use of studio musicians on hit records was a standard practice of the recording industry. The very same studio musicians who worked on the Beach Boys classic *Pet Sounds* album also played on the Monkees records and many other artists. The Monkees eventually fought for and won the right to play on their recordings. There was a rumor that Davy Jones was going to get inducted into the military, but he and his legal team were able to successfully argue that he was the only source of care and income for his father Harry who still lived in Manchester, England. Davy also secretly married, and the news wasn't revealed until 1969, leading to many fans feeling betrayed and abandoning the Monkees and moving on to other Pop stars like Bobby Sherman and David Cassidy.

So, is Paul still with us? Where do you cast your vote? :)

As noted earlier, after checking out some of the clues and fully examining them, I concluded that Paul McCartney was and is alive and well, still creating great music for fans to enjoy. Long Live Paul!

Kit O'Toole

Kit O'Toole is a freelance writer who has written about the music world for over twenty years. She is the author of *Fandom and the Beatles, Songs We Were Singing: Guided Tours Through the Beatles' Tracks,* and *The Beatles, Sgt. Pepper, and the Summer of Love.*

Please give us some biographical information, and a highlight of your work to date.

I am Chicago-based writer and music journalist, Dr. Kit O'Toole. I'm the author of *Songs We Were Singing: Guided Tours Through the Beatles' Lesser-Known Tracks* and *Michael Jackson FAQ: All That's Left to Know About the King of Pop.* I also co-edited *The Act You've Known for All These Years: The Beatles and Fandom* with Beatles historian Kenneth Womack. In addition to my two books, I am also associate editor and a longtime contributor for Beatlefan magazine, reviewer and "Deep Beatles" columnist for *Something Else Reviews,* a frequent contributor to *Cinema Sentries,* and a regular speaker at The Fest for Beatles Fans in Chicago and New York and the Beatles at the Ridge festival in Walnut Ridge, AR. I've also presented at the GRAMMY Museum Mississippi, and written chapters for several academic collections. In addition,

I have also taught several online courses in music history for Monmouth University. I hold a doctorate in Instructional Technology.

When did you become aware of the Beatles, and how long did it take for you to become hooked on them?

Since I grew up in a musical household—Dad plays several instruments—I had been exposed to the Beatles in early childhood. Dad used to play *Norwegian Wood* and *Michelle* on guitar. However, I didn't become a true fan until eighth grade. In chorus class we could bring in any music we wanted to play for the class on Fridays; one day a student brought in the Beatles' *20 Greatest Hits* cassette. Once *Eight Days a Week* blasted through the speakers, I was absolutely hooked; it sounded like nothing else on mid-1980s radio at the time.

What led to the Beatles deciding not to tour anymore? And was that really unheard of for their type of act to do something like that?

It was an unusual decision, since bands toured to promote their latest releases (and it was another important revenue source, of course). But the Beatles grew tired of *Beatlemania* and believed their playing suffered as a result. They couldn't hear themselves over the fans' constant screaming; they were sick of being mobbed; all they saw was "a car and a room and a room and a room" (to paraphrase *A Hard Day's Night*); and they had one too many scary incidents like their treatment in the Philippines. While Brian Epstein objected, the Beatles felt that ceasing touring and focusing strictly on recording would ultimately improve their musicianship.

As the Beatles were now concentrating on albums, and setting new standards in the studio, do you suspect that they cooked up the Paul is Dead rumors as an in-joke?

I honestly don't, although I think they definitely had fun with the rumors once they learned about them. *Glass Onion* from the *White*

Album is the best example of the Beatles having some fun with the rumor, with the line "the walrus was Paul" referring to *I am the Walrus* and the *Magical Mystery Tour* album cover. As I recall, Paul representing the walrus was part of the conspiracy theory.

Do you recall what signs stuck out to you in the songs, and on the record covers?

When I first read books on the Beatles back in high school, I think I read about the "Paul is Dead" hoax for the first time. I probably came across it in *The Compleat Beatles* documentary as well. The "clues" I remember most are on the cover of *Abbey Road*: the "28IF" license plate (I just learned of a Beatles tribute band with that name, which is hilarious), Paul being the only person barefoot, and Ringo supposedly dressed as an undertaker. I also recall two songs where if you play them backwards, you supposedly hear further clues. In *I'm So Tired* you allegedly hear John say "Paul is dead, man, miss him, miss him" or something along those lines. Additionally, in *Strawberry Fields Forever,* you supposedly can hear John say "I buried Paul."

Life *magazine reporters chased Paul down at his farm, and he threw a bucket of water at them. Of course, he chased them down and made amends. This is sort of a one of a kind story. What are your thoughts on all of this?*

Paul probably eventually saw it as a publicity opportunity—as we know, he's Mr. PR! It's interesting that although he does address some specific clues and dismisses them as "bloody stupid," he does announce the breakup of the Beatles. "But the Beatle thing is over. It has been exploded, partly by what we have done, and partly by other people. We are individuals--all different. John married Yoko, I married Linda. We didn't marry the same girl," he said. It's interesting that more people seem to remember Paul talking about the death hoax in that *Life* issue than announcing the Beatles breakup!

The Abbey Road *cover stands out because of the crosswalk alone, but when you see it do you sometimes still look for the signs there?*

As I mentioned above, the 28IF license plate is probably the standout feature. Otherwise I honestly don't think about it that much; I just appreciate the cover for the iconic image it is!

The studio period of the Beatles saw them trapped, but their creativity soared. What has solo-Paul done to bring many of these songs to audiences, with enhanced technology? What do you make of his doing that as a lone pilgrim?

I think it's terrific that he has brought the Beatles' songs to life in a new way not only through performing them, but through utilizing film as an accompaniment. For example, he'll use scenes from A Hard Day's Night to accent songs from the film; for *Helter Skelter*, he uses abstract images to simulate movement of a roller coaster. On his latest "Got Back" tour, he has debuted a virtual duet with John Lennon. Peter Jackson isolated rooftop concert footage of John doing *I've Got a Feeling*, and Paul and the band perform the rest. Seeing an almost 80-year-old Paul duet with a 20-something John brings tears to the eyes.

Some still speak of believing that Paul really was replaced, and Billy's here, so to speak. Do any such theories stick out in your mind?

I remember the theory of Paul dying in a car accident in 1966, and he was replaced by a look-alike actor named William Campbell. Interestingly, there was a story that the theory first circulated in a college newspaper in 1969—Northern Illinois University, one of my alma maters! It turns out that while they did print the story, they were NOT the first.

So, is Paul still with us? Where do you cast your vote? :) You can be a bit cheeky with this answer if you like.

Paul is definitely still with us, unless William Campbell is THAT good an actor. ;)

David Hinckley

David Hinckley worked as a music and entertainment writer with *The New York Daily News* for decades.

Please tell us about yourself, and what you're up to?

I'm a writer who was retired after 35 years with the *New York Daily News*. I spend much of my time now making my wife roll her eyes over my incessant references to Bob Dylan lyrics.

When did you first become aware of the Beatles, and when were you hooked as a fan?

I discovered them in their first American wave, the radio blitz of early 1964. At first I liked them, didn't love them, and since top-40 radio played the same handful of songs about six times an hour, my impatient teenage self started grumbling, "Enough." I remember calling Ken Griffin, then the evening DJ on my local top-40 station, WDRC, and asking him if we could catch a break. He replied, "I know what you mean. All the jocks feel the same. But this is what the kids want now, so we'll wait for it to pass." Happily, history proved both me and Ken wrong. I never stopped liking their early songs, many of which are still among my favorites today, but it wasn't until *A Hard Day's Night* and then *Rubber Soul* that I went all-in.

Did you have a favorite Beatle, and why did they stand out to you?

No strong favorite. I kind of liked John, I guess, probably because he seemed to have a little sharper attitude.

When did you become aware of the Paul is Dead rumors, and what was the reaction of yourself and fans you knew?

Gotta admit I thought they were ridiculous. But silly stories were a part of pop music culture back then, because pop music (rock 'n' roll) was considered a passing lightweight diversion that the kids would soon grow out of, so we could go back to "good" music.

There was almost no serious music journalism, just the celebrity fluff in the *16* magazine tradition, and this felt like an extension of that.

Which 'clues' from the record covers stand out to you? Do you believe they were all unplanned, or was this somewhat of a lark?

I don't think anything was planned. By then you could probably find any "message" you wanted if you looked hard enough.

Which 'clues' from the songs stand out to you, and did you play any of your records backwards?

No. I thought that on the whole, they sounded better forwards.

How big of a commotion did all of this cause among the fans?

I guess it provided a lot of material for DJs or fans looking for a diversion. The people I knew, not really. What does strike me in retrospect is that if a similar rumor arose today, with the Internet, it would blow up into billions of clicks. And really, what else matters?

Some say that the Beatles stopped touring because Paul had been replaced. Why do you think that the group stopped the tours?

I believe their official explanation, which is that they were tired of going on the road to play shows where they couldn't even hear each other, just a lot of screaming. They found the studio much more musically interesting by that point, and the records they made over the next couple of years suggest they were onto something.

Paul brought many songs from the studio years to a stage for the first time, which the Beatles never played live. What do you make of Paul's live performances from these songs?

Terrific. He sounded great and he played them really well. It was like hearing the Beatles concerts we missed in the 1960s. And of course the concert sound technology was so much better by then.

So, is Paul still with us? Where do you cast your vote?

Yes. We still need him, we still feed him, even when he's over 64. Hoo.

Sally Kirkland

Sally Kirkland is an Oscar nominated, Golden Globe award-winning actress whose career has spanned six decades. She studied under legendary acting coach Lee Strasberg, dated her fellow student Robert DeNiro, and had a lengthy romance with Bob Dylan. She has hundreds of film and television credits, and is still working regularly at age eighty.

Please tell us about yourself, and what projects and 'happenings' are you working on?

I've been an actress for 62 years, and have produced many of my films. I studied under Lee Strasberg, along with Robert DeNiro, Dustin Hoffman, and Al Pacino, and am a lifetime member of the Actors Studio. I dated DeNiro in the 1960s. I'm currently finishing three films, one is called *Skeleton in the Closet*, with Terrence Howard and Cuba Gooding, Jr., *Murder, Anyone?*, directed and produced by James Cullen Bressack, and *80 for Brady*, along with Jane Fonda, Lily Tomlin, Rita Moreno, Sally Field and Tom Brady. I am very proud of my starring role in the 2019 film *Cuck*. I'm most proud of being an Oscar nominee, a Golden Globe winner, and winner of Independent Spirit Award and LA Film Critics Award, all for the 1987 film *Anna*. I have 270 film and television credits.

You are no stranger to mysteries, as you had an incredibly memorable role in Oliver Stone's film JFK. *How did that come about, and what are your memories of that experience?*

Oliver Stone has been a friend of mine since the 1970s, and he used to speak to my acting class. My mother was friends with Jacqueline Kennedy. After asking him for a part in *JFK*, Oliver asked me to improvise for three characters, Dorothy Kilgallen,

Kathy Kupcinet, and Rose Cheramie. I stripped down to a teeny bikini for Rose Cheramie, and Oliver hired me on the spot. I am in the first scene in *JFK*. I thoroughly researched Cheramie, and my scene was filmed in Dallas. When I first saw the opening scene at the Academy, you could hear a pin drop in the audience.

When did you know that you wanted to be an actress, and when did you feel that you had made it, and accomplished your goal?

I knew I wanted to be an actress when I went to the Valley Drama Camp at age twelve. I often played male characters, since I am 5'9. I felt I had really made it after appearing in the huge films *The Sting* and *The Way We Were*.

When did you first become aware of the Beatles, and how long did it take for you to become a fan?

Like a lot of people, I saw them on *The Ed Sullivan Show*. I was an Andy Warhol superstar at the time. I was blown away and told my mother, who was editor of *Vogue* magazine, that she had to put them on the cover. They did put the Beatles on the cover. I told her not to tell people she didn't know who the Beatles were, since all the kids knew them.

Do you have a favorite Beatle? What about your choice made that particular Beatle stand out to you?

George Harrison, because of his spiritual path. I've been on a spiritual path since 1969, and worked as a yoga master. I hung out a lot at the Krishna Temple, and loved their vegetarian food.

When did you hear about the rumors that Paul McCartney passed away, and had been replaced with a double?

When everyone else did. I didn't believe it.

Sgt. Pepper's Lonely Hearts Club Band *had a lot of 'clues' on the album cover, leading to the Paul was replaced rumors. - What did you make of the* Sgt. Pepper *album, and which songs are your favorite on that album?*

Some songs on there are *Lucy in the Sky with Diamonds, Getting Better, A Day in the Life, Within You, Without You, A Little Help from My Friends...* I loved them all. *A Little Help from my Friends* is a very practicable song.

Another record with a lot of clues is on the Abbey Road *record cover. Do you like that album, and which songs are your favorites?*

I loved *Something.*

Since you are an established star in Hollywood, did your path ever cross over to any of the Beatles, even after they broke up as a band?

I got to know Ringo Starr very well, and officiated at the wedding of his road manager, when Ringo was best man. Ringo kept popping up in my life. He is the warmest, most down to earth person, no ego at all. Kind, sweet, lovable man. I met Ringo through Bob Dylan, whom I dated for years. I also met George Harrison with Dylan, and told him I knew his wife before he did. That was an incredible scene, alone with Harrison, Dylan, and Lorne Michaels. I met Paul McCartney at one of my big parties, for about 300 people. I never met John Lennon, but did meet Yoko and their son Sean.

So, is Paul still with us? Where do you cast your vote?

Yes, of course he's still with us.

BONUS QUESTION: You were good friends with Bob Dylan. He admired the Beatles, and they admired him. People always ask: what was someone 'really like'. What can you share about what Bob was really like? Not to pry, but in general.

I met Bob when we were both 22, and started dating him in 1975, on and off until 1998. He's been the love my life. I think he's a genius. He's very funny and shy in real life. There were five songs with "Sally" in them. I like to think I might have been his muse. I was dating him at that time, but I will probably never know for sure. He inspired me to become a workaholic.

Patti Gallo-Stenman

Patti Gallo-Stenman is the author of the memoir, *Diary of a Beatlemaniac: A Fab Insider's Look at the Beatles Era.* Worked as a writer for *Vogue* magazine, and as an award-winning copywriter.

How did your interest in the Beatles begin?

As a Philadelphia native, I was a teen in the mid '60s, when I started writing a column for teenagers that launched my career in journalism. I also wrote a diary starting in1962, which chronicled my life as a *Beatlemania*c. I graduated from Temple University and the University of Stockholm International Graduate School, and lived in Europe for nearly 25 years. I'm the mother of identical twin daughters.

Talk about your Beatles book.

Diary of a Beatlemaniac: A Fab insider's look at the Beatles Era, which was published by Cynren Press, is a 2022 winner of the Independent Book Award in the category of Arts & Entertainment. The book is compiled from my diary, scrapbooking, original photographs and interviews. I was also co-president of the Victor Spinetti Fan Club; the actor appeared in all Beatle films.

When did you first become aware of the Beatles?

I first saw the Beatles in a newspaper Sunday magazine during Christmas 1963, then on a segment of the Jack Paar television show on January 3, 1964. Of course, their first appearance on TV's *The Ed Sullivan Show* on February 9, 1964 was beyond amazing. I became a true fan on February 9.

Did you have a favorite Beatle?

Paul McCartney became my favorite Beatle the evening of February 9, 1964 when the group first appeared on *The Ed Sullivan*

Show. His melodic voice, dark good looks, amazing smile and magnetic eyes attracted teenage Patti. After nearly 60 years, Sir Paul remains my Number One.

When did you first hear the rumors that Paul was dead?

Later in 1969 in Philadelphia, I started hearing from radio disc jockeys - where we got most of our Beatle news - and from some university newspapers - something about "Paul is Dead." They said if you would spin the intro from *Revolution 9* backwards on the *White Album* (released in November 1968), you could hear a secret message - "Turn me on deadman." There were other messages, too. Seems Paul died in 1966. The rumors started in 1967, and spread to U.S. college campuses in 1969. The myth also pointed out clues on the cover of *Abbey Road* released in September 1969. These included the Beatles walking over the zebra crossing in funeral-procession style. Paul was out of step and the only one without shoes. This indicated he was a corpse. The license plate on the VW Beatle car on the cover was "LMW 28IF." For those who believed Paul was dead, it translated as "Linda McCartney Weeps 28" IF he survived (even though Paul was 27). Rumor had it that Paul had died in a fiery car crash in England. He had been replaced by a double.

Tell us more about Victor Spinetti.

I was co-president if the Official Victor Spinetti Fan Club of America - Chapter One, in Philadelphia. We got to know actor Victor Spinetti when he appeared in a musical in Philly in September '64. He sent us gossip for our newsletter, and gifted us with Beatle souvenirs. The fan club lasted till we graduated high school in '67. We did not discuss the "Paul is Dead" rumor among us or with Victor, as I recall.

Did you ever play your Beatles records backwards?

No, I didn't, but may have heard a disc jockey playing a record backwards on the radio.

Did you see the Beatles live in concert?

I saw the Beatles as a group three times: On September 2, 1964 at Philadelphia Convention Hall, Philadelphia, PA. On August 16, 1966 at JFK Stadium, Philadelphia, PA. On August 23, 1966 at NY Shea Stadium, New York. The first show was in a convention center where those at floor level could not see much. The sound system was bad, and the screaming never stopped. The second and third time I saw them live were in outdoor stadiums. They looked tiny from the cheap-seats, but the sound systems were a bit better. I cannot recall how many times I have seen both Paul and Ringo solo, but the last two times I saw Paul in concert was in June 2019 in Arlington, Texas, and in May 2022 in Fort Worth, Texas.

Why do you think the Beatles stopped touring?

Why the Beatles stopped touring from what I recall: They were tired of the touring scene. They did not feel creative churning out the same old songs onstage. The audience and numbers were getting out of hand. At that point in 1966, I believe they just felt they were over it. In my opinion, it had nothing to do with the "Paul is Dead" rumor.

So how do you vote- is Paul still with us?

Yes, Paul is still with us. He never left. At 80 or 28, he is still the same incredibly talented chap. I was amazed to see him once again on May 17, 2022 in Fort Worth, Texas.

Robert Rosen

Robert Rosen is the author of *Nowhere Man: The Final Days of John Lennon.* His other books include *A Brooklyn Memoir: My Life as a Boy.*

Will you please tell us about yourself, and your work? Where can the readers follow you online?

I'm the author of the bestselling John Lennon bio *Nowhere Man.* It came out in 2000 and an updated edition is due out in September.

I wrote *Nowhere Man* because, in 1981, five months after Lennon was murdered, I was given exclusive access to the personal diaries he'd kept between 1975 and 1980. The story I tell in the book is the story of his diaries. *A Brooklyn Memoir* came out this summer. It's a childhood journey through 1950s and 60s Flatbush, an insular neighborhood where Holocaust survivors lived side-by-side with WWII vets and the war lingered like a mass hallucination. I've also written *Beaver Street: A History of Modern Pornography*. All my books are available everywhere books are sold. I'm working on a book about America in the 1970s. My writing has appeared in *The Village Voice, Mother Jones, Soho Weekly News, The Independent, Uncut*, and many other magazines and newspapers. I live in New York City with my wife, singer-songwriter Mary Lyn Maiscott. You can check out my Website, robertrosennyc.com, or follow me on social media at facebook.com/robertrosen27, twitter.com/Rrosen2727, and www.instagram.com/rrosen2727/.

When did you first become aware of the Beatles, and did one stand out as your favorite? What stuck out to you about them?

I became aware of them in early 1964, in the weeks leading up to their first appearance on *The Ed Sullivan Show*. I was 11. I write about this in *A Brooklyn Memoir*, which ends with the arrival of the Fab Four, as they were not yet called. The Beatles appeared on *Ed Sullivan* February 9, 79 days after JFK was assassinated. A cloud of gloom hung over America during those 11 weeks. We were a country in mourning and in a state of shock. You'd turn on the TV and it was one long *Dead President Show*. And the Beatles wiped that all away with an explosion of joy. It was as if postwar Flatbush had been stuck in the 1940s. Then the present came rushing in, and suddenly it was the 1960s. The Beatles were everywhere, on every radio, TV, newspaper, and magazine, and everybody was talking about them. You'd walk down the street and hear teenagers listening to the Beatles on their transistor radios. The day after *Ed Sullivan*, I bought my first record album: *Meet the Beatles*. Three bucks in Lamston's. What stuck out was their music. I listened to that album over and over until I knew every word from every song. I can't say one particular Beatle stood out—not then. They were a band, a performing unit, and I knew all their names, which is more than I can say for any other band in 1964.

What was John Lennon and Paul McCartney's relationship like after the Beatles went on to solo careers?

There's one line in *Nowhere Man* that pretty much sums up their relationship. John says of Paul, "I love him like a brother but I don't like him." In the last five years of his life John rarely saw Paul—he didn't want to see him. But he thought about him every day. John was jealous of Paul's ongoing success, the way he pumped out hit after hit while John was secluded in the Dakota doing nothing musical for five years. Paul wanted a Beatles reunion. The idea repulsed John. He wanted to move forward, not backward. John's happiest moment of early 1980 came when Paul was busted in Japan for marijuana and went to jail for nine days. The Wings tour was ruined, and for John, it was an occasion to celebrate.

Did you ever see the Beatles in person, or have any brushes with them during their solo years?

I never saw a Beatle in person, but I've met many people who were close to John. Yoko Ono employed me for six months in 1982 and 1983. I hung out with Julian Lennon for a couple of days in London when he was 17. I met Sean Lennon a number of times when he was very young. I've spoken with May Pang, Neil Aspinall, Elliot Mintz, and one of the musicians who played with John on *Double Fantasy*. You can read about my "gig" with Ono and some of these meetings in *Nowhere Man*.

Was there ever a chance that the Beatles could have put differences aside, and reunited?

Had they lived, who knows what would have happened. But the way things stood in 1980, a reunion was out of the question.

When did you become aware of the rumors that Paul had left us, and was replaced by a look-alike? What did you make of all of this?

I became aware of it around 1969, when I was in high school. I didn't think it was true. It struck me as a good game. Looking for clues and analyzing them was entertaining, a fun thing to talk about.

Which 'clues' stood out to you from the album covers?

Abbey Road and *Sgt. Pepper* were the two album covers that had most of the clues. Let's start with *Abbey Road*, which came out in 1969. On the front cover, a license plate on a parked car says "28 IF," meaning Paul would have been 28 if he'd lived. The Beatles crossing the street are supposed to be a funeral procession. Paul's the corpse because he isn't wearing any shoes. George, dressed in denim, is the gravedigger. Ringo, in a dark suit, represents the congregation at the funeral. And John, in a white suit, is either Jesus or a priest. There's also a police van parked on the street. Police vans are supposedly present at the scene of fatal car accidents, which is how Paul was supposedly killed. Then on the back cover, there are holes in the wall just to the left of "Beatles." The holes look a little like a 3. Hence, 3 Beatles. *Sgt. Pepper* came out in 1967, the year after Paul was "killed" and "replaced." On the front cover, the Beatles are standing in front of what looks like it might be a grave. Somebody is holding a hand over Paul's head. Some people believe the hand is an ancient Greek or Native American death symbol. On top of the grave is what appears to be a left-handed bass guitar. Paul is a left-handed bass player. On the back cover, Paul's standing with his back to the camera and George Harrison's thumb is pointing to the lyric "Wednesday morning at five o'clock." This is supposed to be the time that Paul was pronounced dead. The album opens into a "gatefold," and on the inside cover, Paul's wearing a black armband with the letters OPD, which stands for Officially Pronounced Dead or Ontario Police Department. Your choice.

Which clues from the songs stood out in your mind, and did you ever spin your records backwards?

The clue that I love and had a lot of fun with back in the day is on *Revolution 9*, on the *White Album*. This is the song I spun backwards on my phonograph. If you put the RPM switch between 45 and 33 1/3, the turntable would slip into neutral and you could spin it backwards. When you did that, every time you spun through "number 9," it sounded like "Turn me on dead man." I didn't believe it till I tried it and was amazed that it worked. Then there's the fadeout on *Strawberry Fields Forever*. It sounds as if John's saying, "I buried Paul," though he insisted he's saying, "I'm very bored."

Paul brought many songs from the studio years to a stage for the first time, which the Beatles never played live. What do you make of Paul's live performances from these songs?

If Paul is anything, he's a crowd pleaser and he plays the songs he knows people came to hear. The Beatles stopped touring in 1966 and instead recorded studio albums: *Sgt. Pepper*, the *White Album*, *Abbey Road*. Paul wants to give his fans their money's worth so of course he plays songs off those LPs. Some of his fans probably took out second mortgages to pay for the concert tickets.

So, is Paul still with us? Where do you cast your vote? :)

Paul is living the good life of a talented, aging billionaire.

Vera Ramone King

Vera Ramone was married to Dee Dee Ramone, bass player for the iconic band The Ramones. She is the author of the book *Poisoned Heart: I Married Dee Dee Ramone (The Ramone Years) A Punk Love Story.*

Will you tell us about yourself, and your work?

Vera Ramone King is the author of *Poison Heart: I Married Dee Dee Ramone (The Ramone Years)*. The Ramones' story is tragic and raw, sentiments that could also describe the band's songwriter, bass player, and unsung genius, Dee Dee. A wild ride into the heart and soul of New York City, *Poisoned Heart* is Vera Ramones King's last testament to her former husband, who shocked the world when he died in 2002 of a drug overdose despite having been clean for years.

Dee Dee defined the punk-rock lifestyle. He was a rash, often violent heroin addict, and no one better understood his twisted mentality, or insanity, than his faithful wife Vera. But Vera—herself a less destructive Nancy to Dee Dee's Sid—also came to know the Dee Dee that music fans worldwide held near and dear: a generous, loving man with a soft spot for the less fortunate, who grew up in the tough streets of Queens, New York, and who never stopped working, writing, and performing. He often treated his wife like a Punk Rock Princess, and his greatest joy was the look on his fans' faces as he played them a song. For true fans of The Ramones, those who remember the 1970s as a time of music innovation and inspired creativity, groupies, wannabes, and true music-lovers everywhere, *Poisoned Heart* is destined to become a literary—and rock—classic. For readers too young to have "felt" the electricity of the 1970s, this book will give you an insider's view of that era and will leave you wanting to hear even more of The Ramones. Vera has given us her wonderful book, and here provides her insight to the Beatles and the story of Paul McCartney and Billy Shears. Turn off your mind, relax, and float downstream -and enjoy her insightful commentary.

When did you first see the Beatles, and when did you become a fan?

I was 12 yrs old in the 7th grade and there were a group of girls that LOVED the Beatles! We were Beatles CRAZY!! That winter they were getting tons of air play in NYC on WMCA and WABC AM radio. The Beatles were supposed to be coming to the States for their first US tour and the dates were announced. One of those was going to be at Shea Stadium in Queens, NYC in August. We were trying to buy tickets but no luck. The tickets SOLD OUT in an hour or so and mostly you had to know someone or have a connection to get in. So me and my bestie Pepper made a pact. The radio station WMCA was having a giveaway contest to win a pair of tickets to the Shea Stadium. To enter the contest you had to mail a postcard to the radio station with your name and contact number. If your card was picked they would call your house and you had to pick a Beatle. They would then spin the wheel and if it landed on the Beatle that you picked, you would win the pair of tickets!! As it may be, Pepper told her dad that if the radio station ever called while she was out, that he should pick Paul. One Saturday afternoon the DJ at WMCA radio called Pepper's house. Her father answered and they asked for her but because she wasn't there they asked him to pick a Beatle for "the spin". He picked Paul as he was told and low and behold the wheel landed on Paul!!

Pepper came home later that afternoon and her Dad told her the radio station called and he picked Paul and won the tickets for her to the Shea Stadium concert. But, Pepper didn't believe her father and thought he was playing a joke on her!! After her parents convinced her it wasn't a joke she called me and told me the good news!! Boy oh Boy oh Boy.......when she told me what happened we were both screeching at the top of our lungs, at opposite ends of the phone!!! My parents and siblings had NO IDEA what just happened? You would think there was a fire or something in the apartment! At first my parents said that I couldn't go. I was beyond devastated! I thought it was the end of the world. They said I was too young and thought it was dangerous for two young girls to go the concert without an adult. I was heartbroken by their decision. My birthday was two days after the concert and after weeks of pleading, sobbing, praying and begging they finally gave in and hoped for the best.

The BIG Day finally came. We got there hours early so we could find our seats and waited in line for a couple hours. We got here and found out that a few thousand other people had the same idea. We found our seats but it was high up and we were not happy! We somehow managed to wiggle our way to the front row. We had to sit thru several opening bands like The Cyrkle, Bobby Hebb and couldn't wait for The Beatles to come on. What a show! This was my first concert ever and to see my idols was a dream come true! By the time the concert was over, we were totally exhausted from screaming, the anxiety for weeks and all the preparations to go to this concert. It was the highlight of my life and changed my outlook on everything for me. I discovered my new passion for Rock N' Roll and I was HOOKED. Ten Years later I married my own Paul. His name was Dee Dee Ramone, the heartthrob of the Ramones.

Who was your favorite Beatle, and why?

Paul McCartney was my Favorite Beatle. He was considered to be the "Cute One" and the heartthrob of the group. My bestie named Pepper and I bought EVERYTHING with Paul's face on it, or The Beatles for that matter, that we could find! We bought t-shirts, mugs, magazines, photos etc. There were SO many items to choose from and with all that came the whole fashion thing. You know, the white Go Go Boots, the mini-skirts, London's "MOD" look was BIG at that time. The fashion styles and clothes of the Rock Stars in that era were beautiful and very trendy. I remember I wanted to look like Patti Boyd!! LOL!

What did the Beatles mean to the Ramones? Were the Beatles an influence on the Ramones?

I know that Dee Dee and Joey were definitely inspired by The Beatles' music and style, and Tommy probably, too. Johnny, I don't really know? He once said in an interview that he also was at the Shea Stadium concert in Forest Hills. He said he was in the front row throwing rocks at the band! I don't know if that was really true or if he was saying it for shock reasons. I personally don't think he did that. It's a bit much. You can hear from some of their songwriting that there was Beatles influence in there. Also, the many bands that emerged after The Beatles during that 60's era were very much influenced by them. I'm surprised that The Ramones never did a cover of a Beatles song.

When did you first hear of the rumors that Paul McCartney was dead? Did you and your friends talk about it?

I first heard the rumor on the radio and it was also on the news! What? Paul is Dead? I remember it like it was yesterday. This was HUGE news and everyone was talking about it and discussing if it was True or Not?

What clues do you recall that Paul was dead?

I do recall on the *Abbey Road* cover that supposedly one of the clues was that Paul was barefoot and the others weren't. Then the rumors of the vinyl records when played backwards were various clues saying....Paul is Dead! It sorta sounded like that's what was being said but it wasn't clear enough for me. We would spend hours playing them backwards but not everyone agreed. They released another album after that and I had noticed that they all had New Looks and facial hair. So, it was hard to tell if it was Paul or not? It certainly looked like him but I didn't know him personally and it was hard to tell. Soon the rumors stopped and people went about their own days. On occasion there would be a DJ having fans call in and asking them what their thoughts were?

Did you play your vinyl Beatle records backwards?

No. I tried but it didn't work for me. I didn't know how.

The Abbey Road *and* Sgt. Pepper *covers had so many of these 'clues'. What do you think of these album covers? I mean, so you like the covers/the art?*

Yes. I liked all the album covers. Like others, I would dissect them and see if there were any clues to the rumors that might be true. *Sgt. Pepper* album had a lot of famous people depicted in the Artwork. You really had to study it and look at it with a magnifying glass to see if you could see anything that may give you a clue. Or was this just for publicity? Who would make up a story like this if there was NO truth to it? I guess we'll never know for sure.

Is the following true, or just a rumor? Ringo was at a Ramones after party, and leaned to you and said: 'You know, George had more songs on the albums after we replaced Paul.'

No, but Ringo did ask me if he could have Marky's drumsticks! LOL!!

So, is Paul still with us? Where do you cast your vote?

I'm on the fence about this one. I don't understand why someone would make up a rumor like this for fun? It's very offensive if the person was still alive and in the same band writing songs and rehearsing…whatever. I did see some photos that were online recently comparing the eyes, mouth, ears. Facial features that resembled the "original" Paul but were NOT an exact match when placed over one another. They didn't match up. There certainly would be a LOT of reasons to come up with that scenario to keep The Beatles intact if Paul was killed in a car crash. Also, their long time manager Brian Epstein mysteriously passed away after this. Maybe he didn't want to play that game? They broke up shortly after that and John just left the band. Everything was blamed on poor Yoko but maybe…just maybe, there was more to the story than meets the eye. Someone out there knows the truth but I'm not sure it will be told while the present Paul is still alive.

Charles F. Rosenay

Charles Rosenay is recognized as the consummate Beatles fan, aficionado, and promoter. He began producing Beatles conventions in 1978, which took place in cities all across the country and even Japan. Guests at these conventions included original Beatles drummer Pete Best, John Lennon's first wife Cynthia, Lennon's sister Julia Baird, and Monkees Davy Jones and Peter Tork. In 1980, he founded *Good Day Sunshine*, which became America's #1 Beatles fan club magazine. He was the editor and publisher for fifteen years. Rosenay is featured on a video representing Beatles fans, which airs continuously at the Rock & Roll Hall of Fame museum.

As a result of his contributions to helping keep the Beatles' spirit alive via the fan club publication and the conventions, Charles has had the privilege of meeting and/or spending quality time with just about every Beatle, every member of the Beatles family, as well as associates. He had dinner with the McCartneys, and always considered Linda McCartney a friend. His "close encounters" with George Harrison, Ringo Starr, George Martin, Neil Aspinal, Julian Lennon, Sean Lennon, Alistair Taylor, Mike McCartney and numerous others are great memories, but his one regret is never having had the opportunity to meet John Lennon. Charles F. Rosenay!!! has made many friends as a result of his Beatles-related efforts, and he points to such Liverpool dignitaries as Pete Best and his family, Allan Williams, Sam Leach, Mike Byrne, Joe Flannery and Dave Jones, William Heckle & Jon Keats of Cavern City Tours as his brethren and colleagues in his adopted city.

You have a love for the Beatles, and also the Monkees. Can you discuss the relationship between these two groups?

I love everything from the sixties, but The Beatles were always on the top of my list, followed by The Monkees. When *Sgt. Pepper* came out, and The Beatles got more sophisticated, I was still a young kid listening to AM Radio. With no hit records off "Pepper," I gravitated to the next best thing, as did millions of young people. I became friends with Davy and Peter, who both attended some of my Beatles conventions in the '80s and '90s, and I began co-producing Monkees Conventions back in 1982 and have continued to be involved with them right up to the last one in 2020. I always felt that the stars aligned perfectly and magically when John, Paul, George and Ringo invaded the world. I think that same magic happened with the members of The Monkees - in conjunction with all the great writers whose songs they performed.

When did you first become aware of the Beatles, and how long did it take for you to be a die-hard fan?

For years I have said that my first memory in life was seeing The Beatles on *The Ed Sullivan Show*. It left an unsurpassed impression on me, and I recall walking around deliriously the next day telling everyone - with pride - that I was a Beatles fan - as if I was the only one in the world. Hey, I was a kid! But I knew I was a die-hard fan and it wasn't a passing faze. In retrospect, I probably wanted to grow to be a Beatle, just like girls wanted to grow up and marry a Beatle, but since that was impossible, I guess I did everything else Beatle-related possible: I collected everything on them, read everything I could, started producing conventions to honor them, published/edited a magazine on them, booked and managed Beatles tribute bands, became a tour organizer to bring fellow fans on Beatles trips to London & Liverpool, and pretty much revolved most of my universe around them. I don't think it was surprising that I became a die-hard fan when they became a sensation; I think it's unbelievable that I remained such a devoted fan through the years.

Which Beatle is your favorite, and what about them makes them stand out to you?

Growing up, I recall running around my house singing a riff with only the words, "John, George, Paul and Ringo," at the top of my lungs, because that was the order of which were my favorites. The order changed through the years, but Paul remained my favorite among the "fab four." I specify "fab four" because my personal favorite may actually be Pete Best, the drummer before Ringo! We became friends in the early '80s and he was a special guest at many of my conventions. I represented him for a short while, and we bonded on so many levels. I loved interviewing him on stage, and some of my favorite memories were going out on the town together, seeing a Broadway show, just hanging out. I love his family, and I would be remiss if I didn't admit that he was my favorite because of our friendship. But getting back to Paul, my first "fave," he and Linda were always very nice to me, and there will always be a special place in my heart for Linda McCartney. Meeting Paul was beyond a dream come true, and I am fortunate to have spent so many times in his presence. I am writing this in June of 2022, the month of his 80th birthday and the same months that I have just seen him in concert twice. He is still phenomenal! When those aforementioned stars aligned all those years ago, who would believe that they would shine as bright more than half a decade later?

When did you become aware of the Paul is dead rumors, and how did you react to hearing them?

I was listening to AM radio (I don't think I've graduated to FM) when the DJ announced something about Paul possibly being dead. It was shocking to hear, and my parents immediately told me not to listen to rumors. They said it would have been on the news if it was true. Then it was on the news! Not that he died, but that there were all these clues indicating that he might be! I got so caught up in the hysteria that I played all my albums and analyzed every cover, searching for more "clues." It has continued to be a fascination - how could there have been so many "clues" and "coincidences" for something that wasn't true? I got caught up in a similar web sometime later when a radio station started playing songs by a band called "Klaatu" that the DJs were claiming may have been The Beatles recording under another name. It was similar hoopla, but it faded quickly. I've since interviewed Terry Draper from Klaatu, and it probably gave them more attention than they would have otherwise had, but it didn't last long. Unlike the "Paul is Dead" topic, which we are still talking about now, and is still fascinating.

Which 'clues' on the record covers stand out to you?

Mostly the ones on *Sgt. Pepper*. The car's license plate that reads "28 IF" and Paul walking barefoot stand out. The mirror trick with the *Pepper* drumhead is mind-blowing. Also, the patch on the *Pepper* jacket "OPD" which was the Ontario Police Department, not "Officially Pronounced Dead." For a great overview of these and every other clue, it's worth trying to locate the special issue of the long-defunct Beatles fanzine *Strawberry Fields Forever*, which was published by super-fan Joe Pope (who also produced the first-ever Beatles Convention in the U.S.). The one special issue with the Paul death clues and theories was the brilliant work of Professor Joel Glazier, who also toured with a slide-show presentation of the clues and his observations. Joel was a guest at some of my conventions, and his show was amazing. Joel and Joe Pope have since passed on, but their legacy lives on... as does the "Paul is Dead" controversy!

Did you ever play your vinyl records backwards?

I must admit that my parents' all-in-one furniture unit, containing our black + white television, a bar (which never had booze in it), plus a phonograph, could not play the records backwards. I know this for a fact because I permanently damaged the family record player trying to force it to play my Beatles albums backwards. I had a kiddie record player, which somehow made my *"CHIPMUNKS SING THE BEATLES HITS"* sound great, and I was smart enough to realize that it would snap if I tried to play the records in reverse. I had a friend next door who had a player that could, indeed, play the records backwards but his parents wouldn't let him because they insisted it would scratch the records and ruin the needle. They were probably right.

You sound as though you think that at least the clues were purposefully planted.

It's common knowledge that Capitol Records/Apple had a windfall as Beatles albums were flying off the shelves again. People were looking and listening for clues on albums they may have already owned and were replacing, or never bought in the first place. If this was a publicity scheme by a record executive, he or she should have won whatever award is given to geniuses of marketing. But it wasn't promotional brilliance, it was unbelievable coincidences. What is never mentioned is how many new stereos were sold because so many people broke their record players trying to play records backwards! Did we hear "Cranberry Sauce?" Did we hear "I'm very bored?" Did we hear "I buried Paul?" The only thing that was definitely buried was the broken Victrola!

So, is Paul still with us? Where do you cast your vote?

I had the pleasure of meeting Sir Paul McCartney on a number of occasions. The first time was backstage at a concert in Birmingham, England at the NEC. I was there with pre-Brian Epstein promoter Sam Leach, who booked many of The Beatles' gigs throughout the outskirts of Liverpool before they were at the Cavern Club. He brought his daughter, Samantha, along. I have told the story of me meeting Paul for the first time many times, and it was published in a book about Paul McCartney, but it's a memory worth repeating for me to give the answer to this question. I first started bringing U.S. Beatles fans to England as a host and tour guide back in 1983. I've been doing `Magical History Tours' ever since through my company www.LiverpoolTours.com. Back then, a lot of great Beatle-related people were still alive, like Allan Williams, Bob Wooler, Paddy Delaney (the doorman at The Cavern), Alistair Taylor, John's Uncle Charlie, Alf Bicknell (The Beatles' chauffeur) and others. One of the people I got closest to was Sam Leach, who had promoted The Beatles in the early sixties and arranged for them to play at numerous venues - such as New Brighton's Tower Ballroom in January of 1962.

Sam was a great guy and an interesting character, and we immediately hit it off. He spoke in a very distinct Scouse accent which was very hard to understand because he also had a slight speech impediment. Sam once asked me, "Charles, when are you going to bring me over to one of your Beatle conventions?" I had been producing Beatles conventions since 1978 and he wanted to come to America as a guest speaker. I thought to myself, 'Who's going to understand him? We can barely understand him in Liverpool!' Despite these reservations, I decided to invite Sam to the USA. I told him that because he was such a dear friend, he would be more than welcome to come over as my guest. Sam told me he was going to publish a book and he wanted me to arrange a book-signing session.

In return for inviting him to America, Sam said he would arrange for me to meet Paul McCartney backstage if he ever toured. When he said this, I simply smiled and said, "Sure, no problem." Well, who would have ever thought that Sam could have been able to make that happen, and that Paul McCartney would ever tour again? Although we all know that Paul has been regularly touring since the late '80s, he had taken a long break from the stage at the start of the decade. So, I never believed it would happen and put the idea to the back of my mind. In the meantime, Sam came to America for several conventions in Connecticut and one in Miami in 1984.

Sometime near the start of Paul's World Tour, Sam rang me up and said, "Hey, are you coming over for any of the concerts?" He remembered his promise. I replied, "Yes, I'm bringing a group over to the NEC in Birmingham." Misunderstanding, Sam replied, "A rock group? A band?" I said," No, I'm bringing a group of fans - just like I would normally do in August for *Beatleweek*. We're going to spend three days in London and three days in and around Liverpool, and we're going to go to the Birmingham concert." He said, "Great, I'm going to get you backstage." I did not believe it. He kept saying, I'm going to take you with 'Sammy.' I thought, 'OK, he's losing it… he's calling himself Sammy.' Well, it turns out Sammy was his daughter, Samantha!

It was on Tuesday, the 2nd of January, 1990, when the day of the concert at Birmingham's NEC finally came. We had incredible seats in the third row from the stage. After we found our seats, I remember telling the fellow fans who came with me, "I'll see you later. I've got to go backstage." I don't think they believed that I was really going to go backstage! I didn't believe it myself. I was ushered into a room. It wasn't a tiny green room - it was packed with around 100 people. Paul hadn't done any shows in Liverpool by this stage of the tour, so all his friends and family were there: 'Vera, Chuck and Dave' - all his cousins and relatives; and even his family's neighbours and friends. The concert was due to start at eight pm and it was already ten-to-eight. I was thinking that my dream would be shattered – it was already too late. But sure enough, eight o'clock came, and when the concert was supposed to start, Paul walked into this room and started chatting to people. I said to Sam, 'He's never going to get to us. There's never going to be time.' However, it turned out that there was enough time - even though the concert was scheduled for eight, there was either an opening act or a D.J. which gave people time to buy drinks and food – and it gave Paul the time to meet and greet.

Paul made his way through the whole crowd, and finally spotted Sam. I was next to Sam and his daughter Sammy (Samantha). Paul ran over and hugged Sam Leach like he was his long-lost dad; the connection was amazing. Paul said, "How's everyone, who's this one?" And I was thinking, 'He's talking about me.' But of course, he was talking about the little girl next to me. Sam said, "This is Sammy, my daughter." Paul picked her up, hugged her, gave her lots of attention. I was standing there like it was an out-of-body experience. This was Paul McCartney in front of me; it was a dream come true. And I was afraid of what to say, in case I crumbled and made a fool of myself. Finally, Paul asked Sam, "Who's this lad?" - he was looking at me right in the eyes. Sam said, "This is my good mate, Charles Rosenay from The States. And Paul replied, "How are you? Nice to meet you." I mumbled something like, "Oh, my God, you have no idea how much you mean to me and how much your music is..." - something that had probably been said to him a billion times.

Sam stopped me and said, "Charles Rosenay is the producer of Beatle conventions in the States. Paul said, "That's cool." Sam added, "He brings American fans over to England every summer for Beatle tours. And he's got a group here." Paul responded, "Oh, that's cool." Sam added, "Charles also publishes a Beatles magazine called *Good Day Sunshine*." Paul quipped, "Oh, nice title. So when do I get my royalties?" I thought that was the funniest line! His sense of humour made my apprehension melt away. I smiled and we embraced. Paul said, "Come on, let's get some photos." We then took pictures of the four of us together, of Paul and Sam together, and of his daughter, Sammy, with Paul. Sam Leach had forgotten his camera. Thank goodness I brought mine. Paul said, "I've got to run." And within minutes, he was on stage. Sam said, "Well, come on. We don't want to miss the concert." That was the first time I had met Paul but I have since had the pleasure of meeting him a number of times. I'll never forget the first one. If you're going to ask me about the show thereafter, I really can't answer because I was in seventh heaven over the backstage meeting! I was in the clouds; this was a dream come true. Prior to that, the only time I had encountered my idols was when I had met The Monkees in 1986. However, this day far surpassed that! Meeting Paul was the greatest thing I could ever imagine. My dream had come true – and it was all thanks to Sam Leach. Yeah yeah yeah!!!

But there is a point to all this connected to the question. For one minute, let's just accept the ridiculous premise that Paul McCartney had really been killed in a car crash on the M1 and was replaced by Billie Shears, or William Campbell, or even an alien from another planet. Yes, I'm thinking of the film *Invasion of the Body Snatchers*. If we can somehow disregard every notion of logic, and accept the fact Paul McCartney was "replaced," the imposter would have had to look like him, sound like him, play instruments like him, and be able to fool everyone around him. He would have had to have been the greatest actor in history, as well as one of the greatest musicians!

The new Paul would have had to have years of CIA/KBG/Interpol/ Scotland Yard-level training to make sure he knew everything about the icon he was replacing. How far back could that go? Could this "imPAULster" (Paul imposter) have learned about the earliest years of The Beatles - even before Ringo - enough to have known about someone like Sam Leach?

The answer is obvious.

Marshall Terrill

Marshall Terrill is the author of many books, including *Lennon, Dylan, Alice and Jesus.*

Please tell us about yourself, your work, and what is your latest?

My name is Marshall Terrill and I'm a film, sports and music writer and the author of more than thirty books, including best-selling biographies of Elvis Presley, Steve McQueen, Johnny Cash, Billy Graham and basketball legend "Pistol" Pete Maravich. My latest book is *Lennon, Dylan, Alice and Jesus*, and co-authored by evangelist Greg Laurie. It examines the spiritual lives of rock stars from the 20th and 21st centuries.

When did you discover the Beatles, and how long did it take for you to be hooked?

I discovered the Beatles in 1973 when I was 10 years old. I am a second generation fan. I discovered them when my brother Michael, who is four years older than me, purchased *The Beatles 1962-1966* and I heard the songs coming out of his room. I knew all of those songs by heart but didn't realize it was all one group. When I did, I was amazed. Then I found out there was a second part to that album, *The Beatles 1967-1970* and loved those songs even more. From there, I was totally hooked. And if you must know what the third album was, it was *Sergeant Pepper's Lonely Hearts Club Band*. From there, I was going to Korvettes (a popular department store in the Washington D.C. area) and buying either a Beatles or a solo

Beatle's album once a week. At the time, Korvette's priced their albums at \$4.44 for a single LP and \$8.98 for a double LP. My allowance was \$10 a week, and I worked all week so I could go to Korvette's on the weekends and buy my music.

Who is your favorite Beatle, and why?

This is an interesting question because in the beginning when I first started on my Beatles journey, it was Paul McCartney. He was the most high-profile, Wings was just starting to hit their stride with *Band on the Run* and then by the time 1976 rolled around, the Wings Over America tour dominated the headlines. Wings even came to Washington D.C. and played the Capital Centre, but I was only 13 – and my parents were not going to let me go to a rock concert by myself. It was one of the greatest disappointments of my young life. But as I grew older – I wanna say by high school – I became a John Lennon man. To me, he was the quintessential artist in that he wrote about his life experiences. You knew exactly where he was in his life as his albums uniquely documented his life. I also liked the fact that his artistry extended to drawing, writing poems, etc. Then during his house husband phase, I became really curious because at the time, we weren't getting much information about his life. Then *Double Fantasy* came out, he was making beautiful and happy music and then he was suddenly taken from us. I actually went to a vigil for him in Washington D.C. at the Lincoln Memorial. I remember it as a very dark and cold day and thousands of people crying. I was sixteen at the time. It took me many, many years to get over John Lennon's death.

Do you recall when you first heard of the rumors that Paul McCartney was dead? What was your reaction?

I do. It was in 1976. You might not recall this, but a Canadian rock group named Klaatu released an album called *3:47 EST* featuring a single called *Sub-Rosa Subway*. The lead vocals were very McCartney-esque and rumors were going around that it was a

Beatles reunion in disguise. That also led back to the old "Paul is Dead" rumors from 1969, which, of course, I had to check out.

Did you play your records backwards?

Yes, I did. Specifically *Revolution #9*. My best friend and fellow Beatles fan had a state of the art stereo where his turntable could pause (I still had one of those old-style plastic turntables that played only three speeds: 78, 45 and 16) his turntable. We were blown away that Lennon's voice said, "Turn me on dead man, turn me on dead man."

If Paul had departed, would you say he had a pretty decent run as a solo artist?

If we're going to get technical, if Paul McCartney "blew his mind out in a car" and died in 1966 according to the rumors, he had no solo career. Problem solved!

Which clues stand out to you from the records, and songs?

Definitely playing *Revolution No. 9* backwards and some of the clues on *Abbey Road*. The license plate reading "28 IF" and the symbolism of The Beatles walking across Abbey Road: Lennon as God because he was wearing all white, Paul as the deceased because he was barefoot, George as the ditch digger (I always got a kick out of that one!) and Ringo as a mourner because he was wearing black. Years later when I wrote for *Daytrippin'* magazine, I did an extensive piece on the anniversary of those rumors. That was one of the clips I submitted to a newspaper when I first started writing, and they hired me based on that story – seriously, I have the Beatles to thank for my literary career.

With no Paul, John would have to have written twice as many songs. What do you think of them as a songwriting team?

They were the greatest songwriting team in history bar none. As Greg Laurie and I wrote in *Lennon, Dylan, Alice & Jesus*: "When he

(Lennon) and Paul McCartney matched up, they were without equals. Together they had written approximately 200 songs, many of them iconic. "Lennon would write something like *Strawberry Fields Forever* and McCartney would answer with a song like *Penny Lane*. One was cynical and mystical; the other buoyant and upbeat. They fed off each other and had alchemy that was off the charts. Most of that was lost when they headed their separate ways."

Some say that the Beatles retreated to the studio because Paul was gone. What do you think of the Beatles abandoning the tours, and their work in the studio?

Not only was it brave and kept the Beatles going for a few more years, it was their best work. I find myself listening to the *White Album* more than any other album and their psychedelic years produced some of their greatest music. It certainly added a lot of color to those songs. I loved their studio years more than I did the touring years. Of course, I'd be remiss if I didn't mention *Revolver*" which to me, feels like the start of their studio years rather than *Sergeant Pepper*" I know they toured after that album, but to me, that was the start of something new for the band.

So, is Paul still with us? Where do you cast your vote?

Yes, Paul is still with is. And if that rumor started in the age of the Internet, it would have been squashed like a bug in 24 hours. But because it happened in 1969, it was allowed to gain traction and spread like wildfire…that said, there was something fun about that time period. The whole "Paul is Dead" phase, to me, is harmless fun because of the silly clues. Here we are still talking about it more than sixty years later…and happily, Paul McCartney is still with us.

Leslie Cavendish

Leslie Cavendish was a barber who was envied by all of his peers. He cut the most famous mop tops in the world, and was kind enough to share his recollections with us.

Will you please tell us about yourself, and your work?

I was born in East London and grew up as part of a large and lively Jewish family in Burnt Oak, North London. I was apprenticed to Vidal Sassoon in 1962 who was THE fashion stylist of the 60s, and I became a stylist there three years later. By a stroke of luck, I became Paul McCartney's private hairdresser in 1966 all because her stylist didn't have time to style a certain ladies hair (Jane Asher). I soon began to work on the image of all four Beatles either at the Apple offices or in their recording studios. I was even invited along as a friend and participant on the Magical Mystery Tour. In 1967, I opened my own salon, backed by Apple and the Beatles, at King's Road, Chelsea. I now arrange my own "VIP Beatles Tours" in London, I also lecture on the Beatles and Sixties culture at Universities and Literary festivals and attend many worldwide Beatles conventions. You can contact me on my website about my tours and events www.beatleshairdresser.com. My book The Cutting *Edge* which has many Beatles related personal stories and also includes what it was like to be part of the Swinging sixties in London can be purchased at www.beatlesbookstore.com or www. beatleshairdresser.com and my FB page where all books will be personally signed.

How did you get into the hair game, and rise to the top of the field?

Became a hairdresser after collecting my mum from the local salon (I was 15 yrs) and saw the shop was full of women and he was the only man in the salon, that's when I decided this was the job for me.

When do you first recall seeing the Beatles, and how long did it take for you to become a fan?

I first saw The Beatles on a TV program called *Scene* at 6.30 in 1963 and later a TV show called *Val Parnell's Sunday Night at The London Palladium* 1963 that is when I really became a fan. Also watched them live in 1963 in front of 150 people in a small London club and in 1969 on the roof at Apple.

How did you start cutting the hair of the lads?

It started with Paul McCartney at his home, John at Apple's Saville Row offices and George and Ringo at my shop at 161 Kings Rd Chelsea.

Did you ever come upon the Beatles playing new songs where you were the only audience?

When I was at Paul's house, he would play some songs like *Ob la di Ob la da* which he was going to record (I did not know the title of the song until it appeared on the (*White Album*) also *Day in the Life* being rehearsed at EMI studios (Abbey Rd) and a few other songs that appeared on *Sgt. Pepper*.

When did you first hear of the rumors that Paul was replaced, and had departed his mortal coil? Which rumors stuck out to you?

Only heard the rumors from conspiracy fans mainly from the US so they could start saying is he Dead or Alive! People started writing books trying to look for clues and analyzing everything it was and is B—s—T.

Did the Beatles provide you with their records, and did you ever spin them backwards?

Used to get all the Apple records given to me when I was at their offices in Saville Row and why would I want to spin them backwards, Unless…

Did you notice if Paul's hair changed after the rumors started?

Gave an interview to a US radio station about how I knew it was the real Paul McCartney and this was my answer. While I was blow-drying his hair after cutting it at his home, I know that Paul's hair falls just to the right of middle in a natural fall. I started combing his hair off his face and checked to see if his hair still falls the same way as before and it DID! He saw what I was doing, and I told him that as his hair falls the same way as before he was not dead but Alive. He said "that's good to know" and then we both started laughing.

Could you tell us a bit about Jay Sebring, and what that memory holds?

Received a phone call at my Chelsea salon from a Jay Sebring who then told me about his clientele (Marlon Brando, Steve McQueen, Frank Sinatra, Warren Beatty, Bruce Lee, and Paul Newman etc). Jay said that with both of our clienteles we could introduce hair products and sell them to the public through salons, pharmacists, and department stores. Why don't you come over to L.A. in the next couple of weeks and stay so we can discuss it further. At that time, I was busy with Beatles and other stuff and said to Jay that I will be in touch at the end of August to discuss it more. I then heard on the news that Jay along with Sharon Tate and four others, that the Manson gang had murdered them. I was supposed to be at Cielo Drive at the same time of the murders and when I watched the film *Once Upon a Time in Hollywood* it sent a shiver through me, also every time it's mentioned I often think about that invite in August 1969.

So, is Paul still with us? Where do you cast your vote?

YES-YES-YES AND YOU BETTER BELIEVE IT!

Janice Mitchell

Janice Mitchell is the author of the best seller *My Ticket to Ride: How I Ran Away to England to Meet the Beatles and Got Rock and Roll Banned in Cleveland (A True Story From 1964.)*

Will you please tell us about yourself, your work, and what's new?

I'm Janice Mitchell, author of the Amazon Best Selling book: *My Ticket To Ride: How I Ran Away To England To Meet The Beatles*

And Got Rock And Roll Banned In Cleveland (A True Story From 1964). Published September 2021, Gray & Co. I'm also a nationally lauded award-winning investigator who has cracked major criminal and civil cases in New York City; and I'm a retired Federal investigator. I was dubbed "a modern-day Nancy Drew" by Rikki Klieman, attorney and TV personality, during a television interview. My book showcases the many newspaper headlines and news stories that followed my international adventure that began, without us telling anyone we were moving to England, the morning after the Beatles Concert at Cleveland Public Hall, September 15, 1964. From Cleveland Hopkins Airport to Heathrow – London and Liverpool. And…my friend and I had no idea that anyone was looking for us during our 23-day adventure. But everyone – Scotland Yard, and even the Beatles were trying to find us. I tell my exciting story, including the details of how I planned the journey throughout the summer of 1964, and about the unexpected and incredible encounter with the Rolling Stores, and the shocking invitation I had from one of the Stones. Follow along with me to the coffee bars and nightclubs in Soho and meet the two cute Liverpool lads we hung out with and hitchhiked with to Liverpool! My upcoming events include International Beatles Week in Liverpool UK, where I'll be selling my book and having an amazing interview with the Cavern Club representative, on the Main Stage at the Adelphi Hotel. Additionally, I'm anticipating breaking news about my story. I'm also working on my next book, a true story, about one of my most daring internationally-based investigations in New York City.

When did you first become aware of the Beatles, and when did you become a fan?

I became aware of the Beatles on December 26, 1963, when I heard for the very first time *I Want to Hold Your Hand* playing on my transistor radio while doing homework in my kitchen. I was a 15-year-old Catholic high school girl attending an all-girls school. I became a fan on the same date at that moment!

Which Beatle was your favorite, and why?

I was drawn to George. He was dubbed the "quiet Beatle". He was soulful and mysterious and for some unknown reason I found that intriguing. However, it could have been those gorgeous eyes!

When did you become aware of the rumors saying that Paul McCartney was dead?

Probably 1967 or so when the story started circulating in the news.

Did you scour the record covers, and look for clues?

I recall there were supposedly clues on the *Abbey Road* album cover. Maybe *Sgt. Pepper*, but I'm not positive. I left all the record cover scouring to the experts and the fans who were in love with this theory that Paul had been killed in a car crash and the Beatles wanted to spare the fans feelings, so they brought in a "replacement Paul". Who doesn't love the notion of looking for clues in trying to solve a mystery…and especially one involving Paul McCartney! Anything to keep the fans interest piqued!

Were your friends as big fans as you are, and did you ever discuss the rumors?

I remember talking about this among friends since it was all over the news. We thought it was weird. Why Paul? What car accident? We wondered how anyone could make a joke of someone dying in a car accident. I didn't know of anyone who took it seriously, at least no one who would admit it. The Paul is Dead thing seemed to just materialize out of thin air. But there was no evidence it was true. It was bizarre but got a lot of publicity.

Did you ever play your records backwards?

No. Never. A cringe-worthy suggestion. Records are not created to be played backwards. God meant them to be played clockwise the same as the way the world turns.

Which 'clues' stand out most in your mind?

The one I recall the most vividly is the Volkswagen license plate 28 IF, supposedly meaning that since Paul was 27 years old at the time he "died", the 28 IF means that he would have been 28 IF he hadn't "died."

What does 'The walrus was Paul', mean to you?

Another lengthy stretch of the imagination. Then and even now, the notion that Paul was "the walrus" remains a question to many. It was an extension of the "Paul is Dead" rumor. However, the "walrus" idea was even more mysterious because it wasn't based on an image that could be identified. I don't believe anyone was scouring record albums for the walrus. It was a made-up story supposedly supporting Pauls' death. Very obscure connection to the Greek translation of the word 'walrus' meaning "corpse". Fans thrived on the obscure idea. Especially when it was connected to John Lennon. One of John's favorite authors was Lewis Carroll. Carroll's poem "The Walrus and the Carpenter" was a reference in one of John's songs. However, John didn't read the poem carefully to discover that the Walrus and Carpenter conspired, in act of intentional deceit, to trick young oysters to the shore and then eat them. So, when John offhandedly referred to Paul as the walrus, I suppose without thinking it over too carefully – and not considering how fans and news people would jump all over it. It was the fans and journalists who devoured the idea wanting more and more to explain Paul's mysterious disappearance. The explanation –however was quite ordinary. Poor Paul simply wanted to spend quiet time in Scotland with his newborn baby. Paul was simply spending quiet time in Scotland being dad to his new baby girl Mary and enjoying a bit of family life.

So, is Paul still with us? Where do you cast your vote?

Paul is still with us. He's never left us. In fact, Sir Paul just celebrated his 80th birthday on June 18, 2022, and he's never been better! Paul never was dead. And he never was the walrus. *Time* magazine even included "Paul is Dead" in a story about "the world's most enduring conspiracy theories."

David Wayne

David Wayne is the bestselling author of several books on a variety of controversial topics, including *Dead Wrong: Straight Facts on the Country's Most Controversial Cover-Ups* and *Hit List: An In-Depth Investigation Into the Mysterious Deaths of Witnesses to the JFK Assassination*, and is an aficionado of 1960s music.

Will you tell us a bit about yourself, and your work?

Publisher: "David Wayne is the bestselling author of six books and has collaborated with Richard Belzer, Governor Jesse Ventura and Dick Russell. He has over twenty-five years of evidence-based research experience and his area of specialization is the microanalysis of media events." Me: "I write stuff that some people like."

Did any of the conspiracies you have researched shock you, as they turned out to be true?

Of all of them, I would have to say that the case of Princess Diana surprised me the most – primarily because I went into that one thoroughly unconvinced that there was anything foul afoot. My primary reason for that feeling was the fact that I once read where a professional assassin said that a car accident is the least preferable way to kill someone, because you have almost no control over the outcome – lots of people survive it and you never know who will. But that was before I read a more recent development in the intelligence community referred to as the "Boston Brakes" - read about *that* one if you want to be surprised at the extent of control they now have via new technologies. There's a video available online of a Project Manager of DARPA (Defense Advanced Research Projects Agency), which actually documents that technique as a viable method of assassination.

When did you become aware of the Beatles, and how long did it take for you to become a fan?

I became a fan immediately and I still love looking at videos online of some of their first appearances in the U.S., like Shea Stadium and *The Ed Sullivan Show*. I guess I consider myself a "kind-of-historian" – just from decades of reading about everything I found interesting – and I've enjoyed reading about history since I was a little kid. And I think the most noteworthy thing about the whole Beatles phenomenon is that it was so *totally focused*. What I mean by that is that, nowadays, we just get *swallowed* up into this big massive bubble of everything that's going on all over the place. Looking back at the "British Invasion" as it was called, the whole country knew that The Beatles were going to be on *The Ed Sullivan Show* on Sunday night. Everybody knew it. Everybody watched it. Everybody talked about it the next day. Everybody was on the same page. And things will (probably) never be that singularly-focused again. Entertainment (and everything else!) is now splintered into thousands, if not millions, of separately-focused events and groups. For that reason, it's even *more* amazing to look back at a time when the focus was wholly singular. When everybody knew – *knew* – that everyone cool in the country was going to be watching the *exact* same thing at the *exact* same time. That's not just a major event, as we may have today – that's a huge phenomenon.

Did you have a favorite Beatle, and why are they your favorite?

John, initially because of those great, haunting vocals on songs like *You've Got To Hide Your Love Away* and *Ticket To Ride* and my all-time favorite Beatles' song, *You're Gonna Lose That Girl* (these were all in 1965, when most "adults" were contemplating how to get rid of "hippies" and supporting the horrible war in Vietnam and Laos). I remember finding *You're Gonna Lose That Girl* online a few years ago – with Ringo and his cigarettes, as they put that track down in the studio. I must have watched that hundreds of times, easy – *never* get tired of it. If you search "you're gonna lose that girl studio" it comes up online. With a set of good headphones, that's two-and-a-half minutes of heaven, to me. It's so good that it gives you goosebumps.

Later on, it was more for John's political stance, which was incredibly courageous, speaking up to challenge authority. And then, at a major point historically, which few people even realize, he actually spun off of that. There was a time when extremist groups like the Weather Underground were espousing to young people that they may actually have to kill their parents as part of the "revolution" (that's true, believe it or not!). And then – right at that crucial juncture in the whole cultural revolution of the Sixties, when everybody was wondering how far things were actually going to go – John spearheaded the answer to that with the song *Revolution*. And mostly everybody was relieved at that "peaceful instruction," as it might be called. Because, just as John sang it, everybody realized that it was the right turn and the words really hit people right where they lived:

"But if you go carrying pictures of Chairman Mao – You ain't gonna make it with anyone anyhow."

And then, in later years with songs like *Instant Karma*, he took that peaceful instruction up to an even higher level.

The 1960's really saw things stirred up, and people began to question things. Do you think that atmosphere led to the rumors about Paul's demise?

That's an excellent point. When you study the era of the 1960s, it's really shocking. Dr. Martin Luther King was assassinated in broad daylight, then quickly followed by Senator Kennedy, right after it looked like he was going to secure the nomination for President, then riots and fires, all across the country. They were very volatile times, which led people to believe that almost anything was possible. After JFK's alleged assassin was gunned down in police custody – live on national television, no less – even the sheltered and naïve found that extremely alarming. That led to people questioning just about everything. Trust became a very rare commodity, especially in institutions and the people getting rich from wars and other nasty things. As Richard (Belzer) famously put it: "90% of the American people believe that JFK was killed by a conspiracy. The other 10% work for the government or the media." Or, as I put it once: "If, a few hundred years ago, the richest families in the world all got together and planned out how to stay powerful in the future – we'd have a world pretty much like the one we have right now – totally controlled by the wealthiest." And that's not being a "conspiracy theorist" – that's just knowing history and how to look at the world around you!

On a side note: Bob Dylan also had rumors about his motorcycle accident, and some say that didn't happen. What are your thoughts about Bob Dylan in general, and his accident?

To be honest, I never researched the circumstances surrounding that accident and I don't make conclusions on things I haven't looked thoroughly into. But, to me, Dylan's work was genius. His songs are like a type of modernized poetry – really magical. In fact, the liner notes on the album *Bringing It All Back Home* are some of the best poetry I've ever read. I also loved how whenever he was asked what a song actually "means," he always had the same answer:

"It means whatever it means to *you*."

And his songs just really resonate with images:

"And Madonna, she still has not showed
We see this empty cage now corrode
Where her cape of the stage once had flowed
The fiddler, he now steps to the road
He writes everything's been returned which was owed
On the back of the fish truck that loads
While my conscience explodes."

Which of the clues about Paul jump out at you?

None, to be honest. I never saw any real evidence, other than coincidences, which are inevitable in life. I never saw much of anything there beyond coincidence. The laws of probability are really interesting to examine. There's a phenomenon called the Birthday Paradox which mathematically proves that if you have a group of 50 people, the odds are overwhelming that at least 2 of them will have the same birthday. That seems impossible to most people, since there are 366 possible birthdays, if you include leap year. But that's the way that probability works!

Chance is a very fickle thing. If you flip a coin and it comes up heads 20 times in a row, that has no bearing at all on whether the next flip comes out tails. Probability makes it 50/50 eventually, but only in the extremely long term. People assume things incorrectly about probability.

And the converse is also true. Sean Connery, the "first James Bond," went into a casino in Italy in 1963, went straight up to the roulette table, his favorite game, and started betting his favorite number, 17 – a bet that pays 35-to-1. He lost twice. Then he bet it again – and won – and let all the chips stand on 17. And again – and won and let it all ride. And again – and won. That's a true story. 17 came up three times in a row and he walked away with a small fortune. The odds of the same single number coming up three consecutive times on a European roulette wheel are 50,653-to-1. But wild things can happen in this world – and *do!* You can't make this stuff up! If you put that in a movie, nobody'd believe it! But, like they say, "Truth is much stranger than fiction."

So, my point is, it's easy to get negative and pessimistic about things – like when you watch a movie and somebody gets dealt four aces and you just think, *"Yeah, right!"* But amazing things do happen! And they don't check the odds before they happen, they just *happen,* and then somebody comes along later and figures out what the odds of that were. The odds of getting dealt a Royal Flush in five-card draw poker are 649,740-to-1. And that means that it *has* occasionally happened! So, as it's put in *Hamlet*, "There are more things in Heaven and Earth, Horatio, than are dreamt of in your philosophy."

But I digress. None of the "clues" really stood out for me – I thought it was just another one of many elaborate hoaxes that have been played over the years.

Did you ever play your records backwards?

No. I had too much fun playing them forwards! Younger people won't know what the hell I'm talking about, but we used to play our favorite songs so much that it would literally wear grooves into a record and then it would "skip" and play the same line over and over again until you either moved the needle or put a penny on top of it so that it would play through the groove. And we even thought *that* was fun! But I *have* listened to some of them online, on the original *and* the re-mastered version and, to me, it really *does* sound like "I buried" and *not* "cranberry" – as the skeptics say. Though I would rush to point out that even if it is, that means absolutely nothing. It could just be something completely benign, like bored recording studio people having some fun with us, or just a hoax. I make it a point to look at all the possible scenarios, way before actually using the word "conspiracy" about something.

Paul offered to do a soundtrack for Mark Lane's film, Rush to Judgment. *What do you make of that, and Mark Lane's work?*

Yes, I've read about that. It's much more than that it appears, actually. Mark Lane did some excellent work very early, when people were just becoming aware of all the huge inconsistencies in the official government version of the JFK assassination. Paul met Mark Lane at a party and told him he was interested in his new book and wanted to read it. But it wasn't published yet; it was still in manuscript form. So, Paul asked for a copy anyway and was given a photocopy of it. Then he called Mark Lane a few nights later and – blurting it out bluntly, just said: "Well he could'na done it, could he?"

So, is Paul still with us? Where do you cast your vote?
    Yes.

Tony Peck

Tony Peck is an actor and screenwriter. His father was Hollywood legend Gregory Peck.

Please tell us about yourself and your work, and what you are up to, will you?
    Growing up in Hollywood, it wasn't unpredictable that I became an actor and screenwriter myself. I currently live much of each year with my wife, Paula, in Aspen. As a youth I was a huge fan of The Rolling Stones, but also had a healthy love and respect for The Beatles. Those from Great Britain were never strangers to my family; my father, international screen icon Gregory Peck, had a circle of best friends that included Roger Moore, David Niven and Laurence Olivier.

When did you first become aware of the Beatles, and how long did it take for you to become a fan?
    I became aware of the Beatles in 1963 when I was 7 years old. I used to play *Revolver* endlessly. I was a fan.

Do you have a favorite Beatle, and what stands out to you about them?
    I don't think I favored one over the others. I liked them all together.

Do you have any anecdotes to share about the Beatles as a group, or during their solo years?
    The Beatles played Dodger Stadium in August of 1966. I was 10 years old. My dad was working abroad so we spent that summer in Europe. When we got home to L.A. there was a few months of mail piled up. One of those pieces of mail was an invitation to a party being thrown for the Beatles after their concert. It was at a house

three blocks away from my parent's home. The date of that party, however, was 4 weeks prior to our return to LA. It was a nonstarter for us to attend. But, it still caused me some real pangs of regret.

The Beatles were huge fans of Bob Dylan. Your dad presented a Kennedy Center Honors Award to Dylan. Can you please tell us about that?

My dad was thrilled to have been asked to present the Kennedy Center Honors Award to Bob Dylan. My dad was, above all, an artist. It was natural for him to see the artistry in the work of others. He understood Dylan as an artist. He understood Dylan's poetry, his place in our national consciousness, his importance as a voice for the youth in our country. He saw Dylan clearly. Greg carefully prepared his remarks for presenting Dylan with the award. He worked on his remarks and rehearsed them. I was lucky to be there, in my dad's study, while he was writing and working on those remarks. He read his speech to me, practiced it out loud… changing words and phrases until he had honed his remarks into the concise narrative you heard on the evening in question. Greg put his whole heart into that presentation. Well, he put his whole heart into everything he did. But, I know he wanted his remarks and the presentation of them onstage at the Kennedy Center to convey the great respect he had for Bob Dylan the artist and for this artist as a deserving recipient of the award he was giving. All of that showed that in his remarks.

Did you ever look at the Beatle album covers to search for clues that Paul McCartney may have been replaced?

No. That idea seemed too farfetched to me.

Did you play any of your vinyl records backwards to listen for clues?

No. Not only did the whole idea seem too farfetched to me but I didn't understand how it might be possible to play a vinyl record backwards. I wasn't onboard with the idea in the first place and I definitely didn't want to damage the record player or the needle for something I didn't believe in the first place.

The Beatles, Bob Dylan, and Gregory Peck stood up boldly for racial equality in the 1960's. When you reflect on this, it must make you proud. What do you think of the stances that they took?

I think the stances they took were normal. I know today they, Dylan, my dad, Harry Belafonte, Norman Lear and other clear voices during that period may have been seen as outspoken or liberal or crazy or extreme. But, to me, these outlooks were normal. Looking down on someone because of their religion, the color of their skin, their economic status or level of education… this was repugnant to me then as it is today. It's the way it was in our family; it is how my dad raised us. If there was another way to treat people, I didn't know it. Today I recognize my dad as a man who had the courage of his convictions, as someone who spoke out in favor of religious tolerance, in favor of racial equality, in favor of increased gun control during a period when these ideas were in their infancy. These ideas are more mainstream today although they are no less politically and socially charged.

Which Beatle songs or records stand out to you, and are your favorites?

I love the Beatles early albums. There was an innocence and a romance to them, a purity.

Ironically, really Paul has brought the songs from the studio years to the concert stage. One of his albums was even called Paul is Live. What do you think of Paul playing these songs before audiences?

Having just watched Paul at Glastonbury, you can imagine what the Beatles would have sounded like if they had been able to perform with good PA systems with all of the modern technology. Paul is clearly enjoying it.

So, is Paul still with us? Where do you cast your vote?

Ha ha, I could tell you, but I best not, but he asked me not to tell you!

David Bedford

David Bedford started out writing for the London Beatles Fan Club, and went on to publish his books, *Liddypool: Birthplace of the Beatles, The Fab One Hundred and Four: The Evolution of the Beatles,* and *Finding the Fourth Beatle.*

Will you please tell us about yourself, and your work?

Having had to give up work in 2000 due to ill health, my doctor advised me to find something to keep my mind occupied. I have been surrounded by The Beatles for all my life. I grew up in the Dingle by the bottom of Madryn Street where Ringo was born and attended the same primary/ elementary school that Ringo had attended, though many years later! Since 1989, we have lived near Penny Lane and our three daughters were born in the same hospital as John Lennon and attended the same primary school, Dovedale Primary, that John and George had attended. When Yoko donated a large sum of money to Dovedale I wrote an article for the London Beatles Fan Club, and so began my new life as a Beatles historian and author. My first book, *Liddypool: Birthplace of The Beatles* was published in 2009 and is now in its third edition. I have now had 8 books published, been the historian/ Associate Producer on *Looking for Lennon*, a documentary feature film about the formative years of John's life. I have been involved in so many other projects, too, it is hard to believe how it started all those years ago.

When did you first become aware of the Beatles, and how long did it take for you to become a fan?

I always seem to have known about them, growing up in the Dingle. It was when I started playing guitar that I purchased the *Beatles Complete* guitar book - with all of its errors - and enjoyed playing the Beatles songs. However it was when I started writing about The Beatles that I reconnected with all of their music.

Can you narrow it down to choosing a favorite Beatle, and why are they your favorite?
No - it varies between all 6 of them! (I include Stuart and Pete)

When did you become aware of rumors that Paul was supposed to have died, and how did you react?
I remember reading about it and was amused by it - I love reading conspiracy theories, though I am rarely convinced by any! I read a couple of magazine articles and online features and enjoyed reading them. Always found it a bit of a laugh.

The Sgt. Pepper *album and* Abbey Road *have many 'clues' as did other album covers. Which ones stand out the most to you?*
My favourite is the *Abbey Road* album cover with the four Beatles as the funeral party and the registration number of the VW Beetle!

Which clues from the songs stand out to you?
The Shakespeare quote at the end of "I am the Walrus."

Did you ever play your vinyl records backwards?
Tried to but could never do it properly.

Some people say that the Beatles stopped touring because Paul was replaced. Why do you think that the Beatles gave up the road?
Playing the same few songs to crowds who just screamed must have been terrible for them. They were progressing musically in the studio with no hope of recreating those songs live either.

Ironically, really Paul has brought the songs from the studio years to the concert stage. One of his albums was even called Paul is

Live. What do you think of Paul playing these songs before audiences?

Having just watched Paul at Glastonbury, you can imagine what the Beatles would have sounded like if they had been able to perform with good PA systems with all of the modern technology. Paul is clearly enjoying it.

So, is Paul still with us? Where do you cast your vote?

Ha ha, I could tell you, but I best not, but he asked me not to tell you!

Laurence Juber

Laurence Juber is a multi-talented musical artist who was the lead guitarist for Paul McCartney's group Wings.

Would you please tell us about yourself, and what you currently have in the works? Where can the fans follow you online?

Laurence Juber is a solo performer, recording artist, composer and arranger. His playing fuses folk, jazz, blues, pop and classical styles, creating a multi-faceted performance that belies the use of only one instrument. First internationally recognized as lead guitarist in Paul McCartney's Wings, with whom he won a Grammy®, Juber has since established himself as world-renowned guitar virtuoso and entertainer. Juber, known to his fans as L.J., has recorded more than two dozen albums which spotlight his unique touch and tone on acoustic guitar. His latest release *Select Blends* is a collection of 'virtually live' streaming performances, recorded during Covid lockdown. His *LJ Plays The Beatles* was voted one of Acoustic Guitar Magazine's all-time Top Ten albums. His solo arrangement and performance of *The Pink Panther* theme earned him a second Grammy®, while his arrangement of *Stand By Me* was heard nationally in a *Diamonds Are Forever* commercial. Juber's DVD-Audio project Guitar Noir (AIX Records) won a CES Demmy award for best surround-sound audio.

When did you first see/or become aware of the Beatles, and how long did it take for you to be hooked on them?

Oct '62 hearing *Love Me Do* on the radio. *Please Please Me* was the hook. England 1963, it was hard to not be exposed to them.

Did you have a favorite Beatle, and why were they your favorite?

Liked them as a band, not specifically individually.

You have some albums covering Beatle songs. Will you please tell us about the Beatle songs that you have done, and why you chose them?

I've recorded over 60 Beatles songs, too many to list. Chosen for their appropriateness for solo guitar, as well as favorites, challenges, plus selections by my wife Hope, who produces the recordings.

How did you come to be a member of Wings, and what memories of that experience come to mind? And is it only a rumor that Paul once turned to you before a show, and said: "The best break I ever got was replacing Paul McCartney?"

As a studio musician in London, I worked with Wings' Denny Laine on a David Essex TV show and he recommended me to Paul and Linda.

Do you recall when you first heard the rumors about Paul having met his demise?

July' 79 on a radio interview in NYC with DJ Scott Muni.

What 'clues' about Paul being dead stand out in your mind from the records and the songs?

None - wasn't paying attention.

Which clues from the songs stand out in your mind?

Not applicable.

Did you ever play your records backwards?

Only to hear guitar parts that were recorded backwards....

So, is Paul still with us? Where do you cast your vote? :)

In truth, Paul is not dead but undead - he's a vampire and Wings would only work at night...

Jude Southerland Kessler

Jude Kessler is the author of a huge multi-volume biography of John Lennon, and is perhaps the world's utmost authority on Lennon. The work is projected as a nine volume set.

Tell us about your extensive works on John Lennon.

The John Lennon Series is a proposed 9-volume historical narrative series on the life of John Lennon, including (of course!) his mates, The Beatles. The first volume is a poignant account of his challenging childhood and teen years (his complicated "abandonment" by his parents, the loss of his Uncle George, his mother Julia, and his soul mate Stu Sutcliffe). Then, beginning with Vol. 2 and extending through Vol. 6, *The John Lennon Series* gives readers an almost day-by-day account of John's Beatles years from extensive research that I conducted over 33 years, with seven trips to Liverpool. This secondary research is augmented by hundreds of personal interviews with John's friends and family, professors, early band members, business associates, The Beatles' traveling reporters, pilots and stewardesses, drivers, DJs, and entourage. Vols. 7-9 will cover John's life in the 1970s, his solo career. The various volumes in the series read like a story, but each book contains over 4,000 footnotes, painstakingly supplying in great detail exactly what The Beatles ate, wore, sang, said, and did. Five of the nine volumes are now in print; they are also available on e-book formats. Four more volumes are on the way. You can find out more about *The John Lennon Series* and read sample chapters at https://www.johnlennonseries.com

I know you share a love of The Beatles with your friends. Will you please, tell us a bit about that, please?

Growing up as a pre-teen and teen, all of my friends were Beatles fans. In 1966, four of us even formed a girl-band dubbed "The June Bugs" in honor, of course, of The Fab Four. I was (shockingly!!) the rhythm guitarist, carrying my large, acoustic Silvertone guitar named "Winston" everywhere. "The June Bugs" wrote their (our) own songs, including one potential chart-topper called *It's No Use Pretending* which included this stellar line: "You know you shouldn't lie to yourself/ Cause baby, I'm puttin' you back on the shelf!" Wow. I can't imagine why we didn't secure a recording contract, overnight. In addition to that potential chart-topper, I learned to play four or five cover songs before the callouses hardened my heart toward band life.

The fact that I was a Beatles fan was one of the first things I always told people when I met them; it always defined who I was. And it still does. A few years ago, I encountered one of my former middle school friends at a Christmas party, and I reminded her of our halcyon "June Bug" days. She rolled her eyes disgustedly and snarked, "I've grown up since then." I haven't. I hope I never outgrow The Beatles. They are a source of joy in a dark and contentious world. Today, of course, all of my closest friends are Beatles authors, artists, podcasters, fanzine owners and editors, Fest founders and Fest staff, Beatles convention organizers, members of The Beatles traveling press, members of The Beatles entourage, or Beatles family members. We all meet twice a year at The Fest for Beatles Fans (in New York and Chicago), which gives us two extra Thanksgivings each year! But almost daily, we e-mail and phone each other; we communicate via social media and Marco Polo; we help each other professionally and personally. And we're very close. My Beatles family is precious to me. I only get by with a lot of help from my Beatles friends.

Did you see the band live, or when did you first see them in the media?

I found out about The Beatles just after turning 10 years old. It was December of 1963, two months prior to the boys' first *Ed Sullivan Show* appearance on 9 Feb. 1964. When I stepped off the school bus one chilly morning at Horseshoe Drive Elementary School in Alexandria, Louisiana, several of my friends approached me excitedly. They were holding a Swan or Vee Jay photo sleeve to a Beatles 45. Giggling, they handed the photo to me with this directive: "These are The Beatles!!!!! Everyone is in love with one of them. You have to pick one to "fall in love with" by recess." (What? That's only two hours away! Eeeeek!) From 8:00 a.m. until the recess bell clanged at 10:00 a.m., I studied that black-and-white "grin-at-nothing" (as The Beatles referred to their poses) photo on the front of the flimsy 45-sleeve! And without any information to go on, I hesitantly selected The Beatle whom I was told was George Harrison. However, I could tell from my friends' crestfallen faces that I had failed in my mission. Quite obviously, they didn't expect me to select George. So, I requested a 24-hour reprieve. I asked if I could take the 45-sleeve home for the night and study it. I promised to report back to my clique at recess the following day, having made "a more informed decision." They talked it over for a quick second and then permitted me to delve further. That night, being a studious and serious student, I began to "research" the question of The Beatles. I phoned my friends' older sisters and requested info about the band. I began to gather information. I found out that the group had been formed by John Lennon…that he was the leader of the band. I also found out that he wrote poetry and loved to read. Hmmmmm, right up my alley! By morning recess on the following day, I had "fallen in love" with a boy from Liverpool whom I had never seen in person (or even on TV) – a boy I knew precious little about. I had no inkling that that decision would change my entire life and take me to places I couldn't begin to imagine, meeting people I never even hoped in my wildest dreams to meet. That moment was the beginning of a lifetime dream come true.

When did you become aware of the "Paul is Dead" rumors, and how did your circle react to them?

I was at my friend Pattie Dalme's house in Natchitoches, LA (a quaint, historic town where my family had moved in 1965, when my father had been selected as the Dean of Education for Northwestern State University). Pattie and I were lounging on her bedspread and listening to DJ "Loveable Larry Ryan" on KEEL Radio from Shreveport, LA. That afternoon, Ryan divulged that some "authorities" were claiming, quite vehemently, that Paul McCartney had been killed in an automobile accident. The DJ went on to say that some people believed that The Beatles were covering up the incident, and that a new Paul – a look-alike with an extremely similar voice – had been located and brought into the fold. I can remember Pattie and I stopping what we were doing and listening intently. Then we called Emily and Emily, our two cohorts in crime. A meeting was slated, and that afternoon, we mulled over the strange (very strange!) state of affairs. I can't recall any of us thinking, at that time, that the story was true. Over the next few months, however, as "clues" began to appear on album covers and on backwards tracks of Beatles songs, we were caught up in the "news today, oh boy." And like everyone else, we wondered what was real and what was not. It was an intriguing situation. I remember vacillating between believing the news and doubting the clues.

Did you search for clues, or play any records backwards?

Yes, of course! My friends and I did all things Beatle. We wore Beatles shirts, Beatles hair bands, and Beatles pins. We wrote their names on our tennis shoes. We had their pictures on our bulletin boards. So, whatever "Beatle activities" there were at hand to do, we did them. We even had Beatle-inspired pseudonyms: Luv Lennon and Rain…that sort of thing. None of us were exactly sure how to play a record backwards – without ruining the record, that is – and Beatles albums cost money that few of us had without doing extra chores. So, we didn't attempt this much-touted stunt. We did read the clues in our fanzines. And we discussed the possibilities with some cute boys that we were friends with in a band called "The Square Circle." It was a great way to strike up a conversation! But to be honest...most of my friends were John fans. So, we didn't invest an overwhelming amount of time into this conundrum. If it didn't involve John, well then, we weren't going to fall apart. I know...that sounds callous in retrospect. But remember, we weren't just fans of The Beatles' music or fans of the group as a whole. We were "in love" with specific Beatles. And quite honestly, I don't remember even knowing "a Paul girl" until I entered college. So... while the rumors were interesting to my friends, they didn't seem like "life or death" to us.

Do you think that the band did this as a lark, as it seems to be an excellent opportunity for publicity?

Okay, let me begin my answer by saying that the "Paul is Dead" scenario might be a real occurrence. And for those who believe (which may or may not include me) that Paul died in a car accident and was replaced by a new Paul, this is a serious topic that deserves to be treated as such. On the other hand, I will say that The Beatles are noted for promulgating myths about themselves for publicity and fun. Let me give you one example. During their first trip to Hamburg, The Beatles were initially "assigned" to the Indra club on the "dodgy end" of the Reeperbahn. It had originally been a seedy strip club, and the regular patrons were none too pleased to saunter down to the Indra one steamy August night to find five British boys (John, Paul, George, Stu, and Pete) replacing their strippers. The place was dingy, dark, and unappealing. But the group made their assignment work, and they increased attendance considerably over the next several weeks. In light of those changes (for the better), owner Bruno Koschmider decided that The Beatles deserved a finer venue and promoted them to the larger, nicer Kaiserkeller. While loitering on the pavement and waiting for a van to transport them to the Kaiserkeller, The Beatles amused themselves by deciding to enhance this "promotion narrative" a bit. They decided to "put it out" that "the little, old lady," the frau, who lived above the Indra had whinged to the police about all the noise and mayhem the band was fomenting. The Beatles decided to tell everyone that she was responsible for their being re-located, as it were. It's quite true that residents living in the buildings around the Indra had complained to the police about the blaring sounds of rock'n'roll, but as Pete Best stated in *Drummed Out! The Pete Best Story*, the "old lady who lived directly above the club in an apartment never did complain to the police. She was either deaf or a latter-day rocker." (p. 46) The Beatles had playfully embellished that part of the story. It was a fun and colorful invention, and it was quickly adopted as part of Beatles lore.

I could cite many other instances of "enhancements" that The Beatles cooked up and repeated…for fun. Is the "Paul is Dead" scenario one of these? I have no idea whatsoever. And I'm not taking sides, one way or the other.

Which clues do you find the most interesting?

I think the most artful clue is the tableau that The Beatles supposedly created while crossing Abbey Road (for the front cover of their *Abbey Road* LP). According to many articles, interviews, and websites, the image of the four musicians traipsing over the zebra crossing outside EMI studios was cleverly staged to represent a funeral procession. We are told that John wore white, representing the minister. Next, Ringo was swathed in black mourning clothes, representing a bereaved member of the family or an undertaker. Then, the supposedly deceased Paul is shown in bare feet (not just because "dead men wear no shoes," but also because the bare feet are symbolic of death and rebirth to new life). And finally, in jeans and a jeans shirt, George treks closely behind. He is, we are told, the gravedigger, wearing clothes perfectly suited to the task. This gives the boys' "Why don't we do it in the road?" motivation for snapping the cover photo in front of their studio a bit of an avant-garde feel. It raises the ante from mere "get-er-done photo" to "an event."

In How Do You Sleep *John sang: "Those freaks was right when they said you were dead." What was going on when John composed this song?*

1971 was a great year for Paul McCartney (or whomever). Paul and Linda released their *Ram* LP, featuring the toe-tapping *Uncle Albert/Admiral Halsey*. They saw great success with the single *Another Day*. And personally, they seemed quite content. For John Lennon, things weren't so bright. In a grim meeting where legal documents were signed, John's band, The Beatles, formally broke apart. John refused to attend that contentious occasion because clearly, hurt feelings and anger pervaded, on all sides. It was an extremely unhappy time.

When McCartney's *Ram* was issued, John's pain increased. He became convinced that Paul's not-so-subtle lyrics were digs at Yoko and him. The lyrics of McCartney's *Too Many People*, for example, included pointed lines such as:

"Too many people preaching practices

Don't let them tell you what you wanna be."

This seemed a denouncement of the peace activism that John and Yoko had become involved in. And the chorus of *Too Many People* seemed even more pointed, waggling a finger at John and telling him that he had foolishly "thrown away" the great opportunity of being a Beatle:

"You took your lucky break and broke it in two

Now what can be done for you?

You broke it in two."

John was livid. The implication that John had merely "been lucky" to land in a band with Paul, George, and Ringo galled him no end. And when John heard the oft-repeated lines of *Ram*'s *Back Seat of My Car* proclaiming, "We believe that we can't be wrong," he felt sure that Yoko and he were being cruelly mocked. (Note: These are just some of the taunts that fueled John's ire. Paul and Linda's ads in the music press, mocking John and Yoko, showing them in clown costumes and getting into a bag didn't help matters much.) So, on John's *Imagine* LP, he fired back with his own potent dose of venom in the song, *How Do You Sleep?* One of the lines in that song proclaims, "Those freaks was right when they said you was dead," cleverly alluding to the 1960s "Paul is Dead" scenario. However, John is in no way taking sides on that controversy. In fact, he's not even talking about actually being alive or dead. He's accusing Paul of being

"dead" emotionally, of having no feeling and of being unable to write an authentically emotional song. He elaborates by saying:

"The only thing you done was yesterday,

And since you're gone it's just another day."

John couches his accusation that Paul has limited talent and emotion in the biting reference to the "Paul is Dead" scenario, but John's allegations are not to be taken literally. The two former friends were battling over emotions, motivation, and expression, not existence.

When The Beatles stopped touring, that fed these rumors. Why did they stop touring?

The Beatles' decision to stop touring had nothing whatsoever to do with the fact that Paul was or was not replaced by someone else following a tragic accident. The Beatles wanted to stop touring after they returned from the 1964 North American Tour. George, specifically, despised touring. Paul still enjoyed it, but Ringo thought things had spiraled out of control. He preferred smaller venues as opposed to large stadiums. In fact, a year later, in 1965, Ringo did not enjoy Shea Stadium. In *The Anthology*, Ringo said of Shea, "We were so far away from the audience. They were all across the field, wired in, y' know…it was just very distant. It was totally against what we started out to achieve, which was to entertain, right there, up close." (*The Anthology*, 187) He also despised the constant screaming. He goes on in The Anthology to say, "Screaming's just become a thing to do. We didn't say, 'OK, don't forget, at this concert – Everybody scream!' Everybody just screams." And John fully agreed. In fact, at most of the 1965 concerts, you can see John on stage stomping his feet weirdly and clumsily clapping his hands together with a deranged look on his face. People have mistakenly and unfairly accused John of making fun of people with special needs. But John was making fun of the hysterical, out-of-control fans who were flailing, wailing, gyrating, and throwing all sorts of things at them (including jelly beans, mirrors, lipstick cases, shoes, and once, even a can of fruit cocktail!). By 1965, he had had enough of that nonsense. George, however, was by far the most vocal about his desire to cease touring. George wasn't anti-music or anti-Beatles. He just resented being a prisoner of an increasingly dangerous brand of fame. In Houston, 1965, for example, fans surrounded The Beatles' Electra II plane on the tarmac and held the boys captive for 40 minutes. When the lads were finally removed from the plane via a high-lift catering cart, the fans (still on the wings and wheels of the plane) began throwing objects at them. Chauffeur Alf Bicknell, who was shielding the boys (as was Brian Epstein, Neil Aspinall, Mal Evans, Ira Sidelle, and Tony Barrow), got hit in the face with a Ronson lighter and almost fell backward off the eight-foot-high cart onto the runway. If Paul had not swiftly caught Alf's arm, he would have sustained serious injury. Touring had honestly reached the point of "diminishing returns." And of course, after the backlash of John's completely lifted-out-of-context comments on being "more popular than Jesus" fomented anger and hatred in 1966, touring became even more perilous. When The Beatles quit touring after their Candlestick Park concert (Aug. 1966), they had complied with Brian's wishes that they remain in the public eye and on stage almost two years longer than they wanted to. This wasn't a "Paul is

Dead" issue. This was a "We might all be dead if we keep this up" issue.

When John left us in real life, how did that affect Paul?

I honestly have no idea. Paul is an extremely private person. Paul is friendly, outgoing, and tactful. In fact, he was always the official-unofficial public relations Beatle, widely acknowledged as the peacemaker and "smoother over of problems" by all four boys. But Paul is very protective of his private life. He guards his tongue and his heart – wisely, I might add. The world doesn't need to know how he feels on every topic. Or really, on any topic except the ones he chooses to share. The smart money, in my opinion, is in keeping your own counsel. And Paul does that quite well.

So, is Paul still with us? Where do you cast your vote?

I am forced to say "No comment." About two years ago, I was a guest on a very popular program which is syndicated worldwide. The distinguished host asked for my opinion on this topic, and I gave it. The following week, I received a ton of angry, nasty, threatening e-mails. It was shocking to me that people could be so violent. So instead, I will quote John Lennon: "Whatever gets you through the night, it's all right, all right. "

John Jeffries

Son of author Donald Jeffries. Podcaster and political activist.

Tell us a bit about yourself, and your interests. Has your dad's work influenced you, such as in his popular Hidden History *books, and his podcasts.*

Yes, I'm John Jeffries son of author Donald Jeffries. As far as influence, yes, growing up his unique way of thinking and questioning everything molded me to question everything and have an open-minded and question unjustified authority. As far as interests I've been interested in acting and the film industry and journalism as well as podcasting and possibly pursuing that as a passion and profession.

When did you first become aware of the Beatles, and what did you think of them?

I became aware of the Beatles at an early age. I was quickly aware they were a big part of history.

Did any of the Beatles stand out as your favorite, and what about them did you like?

As far as who stood out as a favorite to me would be John Lennon because he seemed to carry that anti-authority spirit the most and seemed the most interesting.

Do your fellow millennials follow the Beatles, and what other music do they gravitate to?

I would say many millennials don't follow the Beatles or are really aware of their place in history. However I think looking back they should be credited in being the first pop craze with *Beatlemania* and such that swept the nation. Without the Beatles there may have been no Backstreet Boys, NSync, Jonas Brothers, One Direction, or other popular pop bands that had a lot of young fans.

When did you first hear of rumors that Paul McCartney may have died, and been replaced by a double?

I have heard my father mention it, but have no real knowledge about it.

Which 'clues' from the record covers stand out to you?

I don't really know about the clues.

Which 'clues' from the songs stand out to you?

I know my Dad used to play John Lennon's music a lot, and I know there was a line in one of the songs telling Paul: "Those freaks was right when they said you was dead."

Did you ever play your vinyl records backwards?

I don't have any vinyl records!

Some say the Beatles stopped touring because Paul died. Why do you think they stopped touring?

I didn't know they stopped touring, but I guess that contributed to the rumors about Paul.

So, is Paul still with us? Where do you cast your vote?

I would say he is still with us. Like my Dad has said, it would be pretty impossible to find an exact look-alike, who happened to be left-handed, and sang the same, and could write all those songs.

Steve Boone

Steve Boone was the bassist for and a founding member of the Lovin' Spoonful, who had seven straight Top 10 hits in the 1960s, including *Do You Believe in Magic* and *Summer in the City.* He was inducted into the Rock and Roll Hall of Fame along with the rest of the band in 2000.

Please tell us about yourself, and your work.

I am anxious to get back on stage performing the Spoonful music for audiences that are looking forward to re-visiting a favorite time in their lives thru music. I also continue to write and record new music and that is proceeding nicely. Creating an audio/video backdrop for live concerts that will be a living history of Lovin' Spoonful's emergence as a band very influenced by folk and blues standards producing Top 20 chart positions for our first 8 45 rpm releases. *Summer in the City* has attained an evergreen status and has been used in several movies including the Bruce Willis *Die Hard* series.

When did you first see the Beatles, and how long did it take for you to become a fan?

The Ed Sullivan Show was my first impression of Beatles music although their arrival in US was on the news b4 ES show.

Did the Beatles have an effect on your work, and that of your band?

Of course the Beatles had an effect on the Lovin' Spoonful and our music reflected the fact that like the Beatles we wrote our songs and played on the recordings.

Did you have a favorite Beatle, and why did they stand out to you?

I would not be able to name a favorite as the criteria is too broad and each Beatle had their own unique personality that was special.

When did you first hear of rumors that Paul may have been replaced by a look-alike?

Those rumors were not taken seriously by the people I hung out with and if he was truly dead it could not have been effectively kept a secret especially with the inquiring minds on Fleet Street.

Which 'clues' from the record album covers stand out in your mind?

I did not place much interest in furthering this charade as it seemed like a publicity stunt that the Beatles did not need to do. In many ways this type of journalism contributed greatly to what social media platforms like QAnon purports to be actual news and not just media speculation for circulation or click bait. All of social media should be taken with a giant grain of salt.

Which 'clues' from the songs stand out to you?

I did not take the rumors seriously about Paul's death and so did not follow any of the breadcrumbs that were scattered about in the press.

Did you ever play any of your vinyl record albums backwards?

Yes, just for fun because I had a turntable that could be wired to rotate CC/wise.

Some say that the Beatles stopped touring because Paul was gone. What do you think led the Lads to stop touring?

Touring in the early to mid 1960's was not well supported by stage gear and equipment and the media crush the Beatles generated made life on the road for the Beatles like a cloistered existence and I would believe not an enjoyable pursuit.

So, is Paul still with us? Where do you cast your vote?

Paul wondered if we would still like him when he's 64 and despite his omnipresence in the rock hierarchy of the 1960's he still continues to put out new material and for that he should be applauded and encouraged. Yes, Paul is still with us and that is a good thing although I am still waiting on that right hand model Hofner bass he promised me in the dressing room at Shea Stadium in August 1966.

Terry Crain

Terry Crain is a recognized expert on all the Beatles' merchandise that was peddled at the height of *Beatlemania*. Author of the book *NEMS and the Business of Selling Beatles Merchandise in the U.S. 1964-1966*.

Tell us about yourself.

I am a Beatles author and researcher. My book, *NEMS and the Business of Selling Beatles Merchandise in the U.S. 1964-1966* is now in its second edition. The book is about the approximately 150 licensed items that dotted store shelves and helped fuel the band-crazed fan during the time right after the band landed in America and performed on *The Ed Sullivan Show*. Toys, games, dolls, jewelry, clothing, wigs, and more! I am also getting more and more interested into Beatle novelty records from 1963-1966. In fact, my research might be leading to a book about this genre...this wry twist to another Beatles subject matter.

When did you first become aware of the Beatles?

I was 8 years old when they were on *Ed Sullivan*. My older sister had all the records, and she had the "George" Remco doll which I remember watching me every time I was in her room. That doll started my interest and passion for memorabilia items.

How did you first hear the "Paul is Dead" rumors?

Starting in 1967 but taking off in 1969, the *Drake Times-Delphic* published "Is Beatle Paul McCartney Dead?" Then you had rumblings at Ohio Wesleyan University about the story, which later spread to Eastern Michigan University. Detroit disc jockeys joined the momentum and started taking calls on the air about it, even calling Apple Records in London for a denial. Then University of Michigan students started writing papers about it, students at Michigan State researched additional clues, and New York disc jockeys began taking calls from the "Paul McCartney Dead Society." Follow that with Detroit and New York stations broadcasting special reports on the controversy. When ABC's *Contemporary Radio* and the *Chicago Sun-Times* debated the "Paul McCartney Dead? Campuses Swept by Beatle Rumor," it became national news.

When the rumors started building momentum in 1969, I would have been an impressionable 13-year-old. I seemed to get absorbed in everything I did at that time. The Paul is Dead rumor was no exception. I don't remember when I heard about it (no Internet or social media), but somehow, I got the news. I immediately started looking over magazines at the local supermarket that ran articles about the clues, pouring over and detailing every lead with a youthful fascination.

What were some "clues" that you can recall?

Looking back, I realize that the research into clues and the subject had an exciting and unintended byproduct on me. I remember reading about other cultures and their ritual, symbolisms, exotic places, and religious protocols and traditions. My emersion into this topic would have never happened to me if it had not been for the "Paul is Dead" clues. Hand over the head, black roses, flowers, and other symbols led me to other worlds and cultures.

Where do you come down on this - is Paul still alive?

I quickly dismissed the rumor over the months, realizing all of this was farfetched. But my interest in other cultures, countries, and ceremonies stayed with me. I never thought of this aspect until this exercise. How cool it was!

Antony Rotunno

Antony Rotunno is the host of the *Glass Onion* podcast, devoted to exploring the life of John Lennon. He is an accomplished musician who has covered many Beatles songs in his work.

Please tell us about your work, with your delightful books and podcasts, will you?

Well, I'm currently working on a book but haven't been published. I do have a blog with a few Beatles items on it, but my main Beatle-related output is a podcast called *Glass Onion: On John Lennon*, which I started in early 2019. I was absolutely amazed at the time that there wasn't a John Lennon podcast. There were and are a few Paul McCartney ones, obviously because he's still an active artist and he's had a lot more work out there than John for unfortunate reasons, and there are a lot of Beatles podcasts, but I thought I had to plug the John Lennon gap. So my podcast is really about the music and psychology and life of John Lennon, but the way I've managed to extend it is by using John, the events of his life and the years in which they occurred as a launching-off point to talk about other popular culture, psychology in general, politics, society, drugs and many other topics. I've been involved with Internet-based alternative media for a while, around 15 years now, and it's interesting how quite a lot of John Lennon's quotes and observations concur with the alternative movement now. I have another podcast called *Life And Life Only*, which explores life from many different angles, and John Lennon occasionally gets mentioned there as well.

When did you become a Beatle fan?

I became a Beatles fan when I was about 13 or 14. I was born in 1975 so we're talking the late 1980s. Obviously they had been around in my life, so to speak, because if you grow up in England or America it's impossible not to at least be aware of the Beatles. I remember doing a project on them at school, but really the catalyst was my older sister Marina bringing home an album called *A Collection of Beatles Oldies But Goldies*, which was a collection of Beatles singles and other songs from 1963-66. Marina was a big music fan as the whole family were and she played us this record, on vinyl then of course, and we were all quite flabbergasted by the sheer energy and vitality of it. I think we knew the songs but hearing them all together without a pause was quite something, especially since 80's pop songs tended to be quite long, drawn-out and a bit self-conscious. These early Beatles songs had incredible economy, never wasting a second, but even within the 3-year time span there were also massive changes, for example between *She Loves You* and *Eleanor Rigby*, songs which sounded unrecognizable as coming from the same band. I also noticed that every song seemed to have something different, whether it was *I Feel Fine* with the feedback at the start or some different vocal effect, either sped-up or slowed-down. There was constant invention.

Who is your favorite Beatle, and why?

Well, the one I've always identified with the most is John Lennon. Let me preface that by saying that I've always been very comfortable with the idea that John and Paul were absolutely perfectly equal. I've never felt that one was better or more important to the group than the other, because they had clearly discernible strengths and weaknesses. The first John Lennon book I got, also from Marina, was the Ray Coleman biography that I'm now quite critical of but which was a great gateway drug in terms of basic information and introducing to me an incredible character who went through numerous phases and journeys in his life. The other thing was that of course at some point I realized that he wasn't around, and we have to be honest and say that when people die prematurely there is a certain mystique about them. Paul McCartney I believe is somewhat overexposed and he's always been around so never had quite that mystique. It wasn't just that though, it was all the same qualities that others have recognised. There was the enigmatic character, how different he was at different stages of his life, how unique he was and, a bit of a cliche now, the honesty. I do believe that he was quite honest about his failings though I think he was doing it for his own reasons and not necessarily for the good of the world. Having said that, I think the peace campaign was sincere People are complex anyway, and he's among the most complex.

When did you become aware that there was a rumor about Paul McCartney being dead?

I don't remember the exact time I heard about this rumor. I do remember a radio documentary on him and I think he mentioned it at that point and obviously played it down, but I think it just came up at some point during my Beatles immersion. I had a period of about three or four years where I was just absorbing everything, but I don't remember a specific moment.

Did your circle of friends that were Beatle fans discuss any of these rumors? Or did you discuss them later when you became established as a Beatle pundit?

Yes. I had a friend who I shared a flat with in London when I was in my 20s. He was very interested in alternative media and conspiracy culture, and he opened my eyes to lots of things that have proved to be true and are not in fact theories but just don't get any play or are laughed at in the mainstream media. He didn't say that it was definitely true but like me was just a curious person trying to keep an open mind. There were already websites springing up in the 1990s as the Internet started to emerge. I didn't believe it, I just thought it was quite interesting. As for my punditry, I get asked about it sometimes when I appear on other shows. I think there's a belief among the Beatles community that I'm some kind of 'conspiracy hobbyist,' but really I'm just someone who is aware of proven agendas at play in the world and likes to investigate them. I've never brought up P.I.D, just talked about it when asked about it.

When you mull all of this over, do you think that the Beatles did this as a lark?

No, I honestly don't think they were involved. I know that there's a line in the song *Glass Onion* that says 'the walrus was Paul', but that was probably just a reference to him wearing that costume in the *Magical Mystery Tour* film. Also, the Beatles were jokers, especially Lennon, and he liked to mess with people's heads, including the fans.

Which clues jump out at you the most, or that you find the most interesting?

Well, I think the 'I buried Paul' at the end of *Strawberry Fields Forever* is interesting. We know it's not true now because on the *Anthology 1* album outtake, John enunciates the 'cran' of 'cranberry sauce' very clearly and in a more exaggerated way. The clue is interesting though because it's an example of how if you think you're going to hear something and are prepared to hear it, your brain tells you that's what you heard, which happened with me the first time.

Another interesting and quite spooky clue is the fact that there's a hand above Paul's head on the *Sergeant Pepper* cover, twice in the *Magical Mystery Tour* booklet and then once on the *Yellow Submarine* album cover (John's hand this time). On the *Pepper* cover, the hand is obscuring the person directly behind Paul, who is

Stephen Crane, who wrote a short story called *The Open Boat,* which is a story of four men who survive a shipwreck and have to find their way back to shore but only three of them survive. I'm not saying there's anything in it but it's very curious.

In the 1960's, there was a tremendous amount of tumult. Which events stand out to you from that era of change?

I've been doing a series about John Lennon in certain years of his life, and the news events tend to be dominated by the Vietnam War. So I would say that and the 3 high-profile assassinations (4 if you include Malcolm X), those of John F. Kennedy, Martin Luther King and Robert Kennedy. In terms of change, of course there were positive changes and for a while a genuine new feeling, but having studied Vietnam quite a lot, it stands out because I think it tells you so much about how the world is run in terms of high-level capitalism and in terms of power. It's also a great lesson about the media because it woke a lot of the public up at the time about the darker sides of U.S. foreign policy, but I think the main lesson the establishment learned from Vietnam was not to show too much blood and guts to the public on the television. If you take Iraq 2003, it was relatively bloodless if you only saw it on the news, though of course the reality was horrendous and a total scandal. Obviously the Beatles were a huge part of the decade, but it's interesting doing these years in John Lennon's life because you suddenly realize that the psychodrama of his and the Beatles' lives really pale into insignificance when you're actually talking about civil rights, race riots across America and mass bloodshed in the Vietnam War. However, it's interesting to look at those two sides within their own context.

Some say that the Beatles stopped touring because Paul was gone. Why do you think the Beatles stopped touring?

I'm going to follow the fairly well-trodden line here. I think the Beatles just stopped touring because they were absolutely sick of it.

There's a very good documentary called *Beatlemania* from the Timewatch series in England, and one of the lines in it is that the modern touring industry was invented the day after Candlestick Park, which was the Beatles last concert as a touring band. I think what they were trying to say is that all the trauma and troubles that the Beatles went through on their tours forced things to change, so they benefited everyone that came after them. If you actually look at their American touring years, aside from the fairly sanitized version of events in Ron Howard's *Eight Days A Week* film, there were an airplane that caught fire, a woman who'd supposedly predicted Kennedy's death and then predicted that the Beatles would die in a plane crash, a concert where it was raining and the roof wasn't very well covered so there was a chance they could have been electrocuted, and of course the firecracker incident in Memphis that happened in the wake of the 'Bigger Than Jesus' controversy. I could go on but those were a few things, plus the fact that the music wasn't being heard and they were deteriorating as musicians. So I think those were the reasons.

So, is Paul still with us? Where do you cast your vote? :)

In conclusion, I don't think he died in 1966 but I would not be at all surprised if doubles had been employed at some point. I do have a few other things to say about this. There was a big physical change in Paul McCartney at a certain point. I've seen a side-by-side photo where the left side is a screen shot of him in the interview they did just after Manila, so that's Summer '66, and the other side is another screen shot of him giving quite a rambling interview where he looked and sounded quite stoned, from around February '67. In that 8 or 9 month span he looks markedly different but that's partly because he's lost a lot of weight and I believe that John and Paul may well have been doing speedballs, which is a mixture of cocaine and heroin, during the *Sergeant Pepper* sessions, possibly George as well. We do know for a fact, through Joe Goodden's book *Riding So High*, that Robert Fraser was bringing these potent concoctions to the sessions, and Goodden says that some of the Beatles' entourage partook of them. I think excessive cocaine, LSD or heroin use (or indeed all 3 at the same time) can produce profound physical changes, quite like the ones we saw in John Lennon in the same period. I have another side-by-side, of John from the *Revolver* sessions to the *Sgt. Pepper* launch party about a year later and it's hard to believe it's the same person. I think an interesting experiment, which I don't

have the time or inclination to carry out myself, would be to imagine a 'John Is Dead' or 'George Is Dead' rumor from the same time and see if clues can be found. Finally, I would say that the more outlandish conspiracy theories may well be planted in the media to basically ridicule and discredit the idea that the world is very different from what is presented in corporate media. The whole edifice, the 'house of cards,' depends on the majority of the population being kept innocent of how the world really works.

William Matson Law

William Matson Law is one of the leading experts on the medical evidence in the JFK assassination, and author of *In the Eye of History* and other books.

Please tell us about yourself and your work, will you? What projects are you working on now?

A: I started getting into serious research on the JFK assassination 30 years ago when I first read David Lifton's book, *Best Evidence*. As I looked at the autopsy pictures -- of the back of the head, the stare of death, and the others that were contained in the book -- even to my untrained eyes, something told me that something wasn't right. So, I bought the book, took it home, and I read it. I thought this has got to be total garbage. I'd never heard any of this stuff before: the body coming in in a shipping casket and that sort of thing. I thought the whole thing was preposterous. This intrigued me so much that I read the book over several times, and then I started reading everything I could on the Kennedy assassination. When I got tired of reading books, because the information began to be repetitive, I started calling people. I went to Texas to go to a conference that I'd found out about. And that was the journey. And while I was there, I was asked by the head of the conference, George Michael Evica, if I would like to speak on it, because I'd had lunch at the same table on one of the days of the conference. So, that's how the whole thing started. Now, you must understand that I had been reading about this, studying this, and thinking about it every day -- basically driving myself and my family nuts with it, especially my son, who was a teenager at the time. It's been quite a journey, and that led to my doing other books. I think I'm the first person to ever do a book with one of the members of the Kennedy Honor Guard casket team, Hugh Clark. I did a book for him on his experiences. I was told by someone that while you're studying the president and what happened to him, you're going to fall in love with Bobby. And I did. But what they didn't know is that I'd already fallen in love with Bobby Kennedy. After I finished *In the Eye of History*, I decided to try to do the same thing and delve into Bobby's murder. We can talk a little bit about that in a bit.

What was your first memory of seeing the Beatles? How long did it take to become a fan?

My first memory of seeing the Beatles -- I'm sure I saw them before this, and I knew who they were -- but my first real memory is of being in my sister's bedroom. And she was extremely excited because she had just gotten a picture, I believe, out of a package of bubblegum. The bubblegum came with a card that showed all four Beatles. She was very excited about this. I wasn't sure why she was excited, but only a teenage girl can tell you that. That's my first clear memory of the Beatles. There are others, of course, as the years went by. I joined a choir because when they came to our school, the junior high or the high school, I can't remember now, they sang "Sgt. Pepper's Lonely Hearts Club Band," and it was really good.

They said at the end of the program, if you want to do this when you get into junior high, then come see us. So, I did that, and I actually joined the choir instead of band or anything like that because I wanted to be able to sing like that. I never could reach the goal, however.

Did any Beatles personally make them your favorite? What was it about them that made them stick out to you?

I liked, I think, Ringo the most because he seemed to be the most approachable. He looked like the average guy, and he was a little goofy. He was not quite so serious, I think, as the rest of the Beatles. At least that's the way I took it. For some reason, I liked him the most. Even today, I tease my wife when I get in the car. I have a beard and long hair. I get in the car, and I have this little pair of round sunglasses. I always take them off after I put them on, and I say, Ringo is in the building, love. She likes that. That goes back to my fondness for Ringo.

The record albums feature different clues, leading many to believe that Paul was replaced by a double? What were your favorite clues?

The clues on the supposed death of Paul McCartney -- Probably the most that's interesting is the cover of *Sgt. Pepper*, where there's all these supposed clues with the bloody glove on one side and a car on the other. There's the Beatles from the old days in the 60s, and then the new version when that album came out, and the supposed flowers at the bottom representing Paul, representing John's flowers on his grave, I think is how it goes. There're all kinds of things. I like the idea of if you play the album backwards, it says, "Turn me on dead man." That sort of thing.

Song Lyrics also were said to explain that Paul was gone and possibly replaced by Billy Shears, what lyrics stood out to you?

Lyrics that stand out to me in song -- There are many, but the ones that stand out are pieces like, he blew his mind out in a car, and the lyric where he says about the walrus, I think it goes, I said I was the walrus, but the walrus was Paul. I might have that backwards.

Played backwards, messages were relating to the demise. Did you spin your records backwards?

There are all kinds of things about the Beatles and the clues to Paul's death. The argument with one of the other Beatles that caused him to get into his car and drive off into the night, and then he had this tragic accident and was killed. Because they didn't want the public to know that Paul was dead, the Beatles got together with their government, and the government helped them to cover the whole thing up supposedly because people over there would freak out. It's really interesting. The Beatles were brilliant guys, especially John Lennon. I don't understand why it continued, but it did. If anybody had any fun with it, it was probably John Lennon. Of course, there's the famous picture of them going across the street and Paul is the one without shoes, and so that makes him the one that's being buried. One of them is the mortician and one is the undertaker, and that sort of thing. Then there's the Volkswagen Beetle in the background, signifying a beetle apart.

Tell us about your work in a real conspiracy. Please describe events relating to the loss of President Kennedy.

It's a fun thing for people to become invested in. I can certainly see why it would be. People want to believe in conspiracy theories. They do. The shocker is, although most conspiracy theories, not all, are bizarre and pretty strange, you go, "Well, that couldn't possibly be true." Then you get into things that I've delved into like John Kennedy and things like that, and you grasp that sometimes conspiracies are real. I believe there was a conspiracy in the murder of John Kennedy, and that's because I talked to people that had their hands on his body. I went to seek them out. They didn't seek me out. I sought them out and I asked them questions. So, it wasn't like they're running around looking for attention. If anything, they're probably, even at that point when I interviewed them, were tired of it. When you talk to people in the plaza, they just tell the story as they know it. A lot of them want to stay away from talk of conspiracy. They know they're going to get asked, but they try to stay away from that.

You also have researched the loss of Bobby Kennedy. Please tell us about what you have found in that area.

I've started working on a book on and off for 17 years that I'm calling "Shadows in Light." I've written two other books from the time that I started this one until I'm finally finishing it up 17 years later. Part of the reason it's taken me so long was I was really affected by Robert Kennedy's death. Not so much when it happened when I was a kid, but as I grew up and started reading about him, learning about him, and understanding the real loss to the country as a whole and just us as a people. I believe Bobby Kennedy really was what they thought John Kennedy was. Bobby grew into that person. When he first started out with his brother, they called him the little bastard. He was a black and white, heaven or hell guy. I believe it took his brother's death, to this soul crushing experience to really make him understand other people's pain.

He wasn't just a rich kid who lived off his father's money. He came to understand the plight of the average person and the poor and the downtrodden in his own country. His own pain made him see what other people that weren't in his position saw daily. It made him an empath to feel their pain. I believe he lived with that until the last breath that he took. When I talk about Bobby Kennedy, it's not the Bobby Kennedy of his brother's campaign years that I think about. It's the Bobby Kennedy who laid there in a pool of his own blood on a dirty pantry kitchen floor that I mourn, because I know what this country lost when Bobby Kennedy was killed. I've been delving into that. It's been a painful experience for me. I got to go into the archives at some point in my research because I had befriended Lynn Mangan, who was Sirhan Sirhan's private researcher. As we know, Sirhan has been accused of being the assassin of Robert Kennedy. I got to know her and, she took me with her, along with my friend filmmaker Mark Sobel, into the archives. Here they house all the materials from the assassination -- the gun, the clothing people were wearing when they were shot, polka dot dresses that were found, all the evidence from the trial, bullet casings, pieces of bullets. They even have a small vial that contained bones from Robert Kennedy when they had him in surgery.

I was all enthusiastic about going in and seeing the materials, because I thought if I could get near this stuff, it would give me some sort of real insight into this. To my utter dismay, when I got in the room, and they started bringing out the evidence and we were looking at the gun and the bullets, looking at the shell casings, and looking at the pieces of bullet, my whole attitude changed. The air felt heavy. It felt oppressive in the room. I at one point got so weak in the knees that I had to sit down. It was the last place I wanted to be. I was all enthusiastic about maybe I could touch the gun. That would give me something that I always refer to it as touching history. I could touch this historical artifact. When I'm in front of that and I'm seeing all that, it took all I could do to just take pictures of the items, and touching it was the furthest thing from my mind. I didn't want to touch anything because it just made me … I just wanted to run from the room. I wanted to leave that room and not enter it. But I had to stick it out for historical purposes.

Here was my chance. So, I stayed, and my friend and fellow filmmaker Mark Sobel was filming all the stuff. It turned out to be quite an experience, but not in the way I had thought it would be. It was a totally different thing, and I still can't explain it. The heaviness of the air was just incredible to me. It became very personal. And later when I told this to Mark Sobel after it was over, I said, "You're going to think I'm crazy. But the air felt heavy. I didn't feel like I should be in the room."And he looked at me and said, "No, no William, I understand totally. I felt the same way. I felt it was totally wrong for us to be there." I mean, I'm glad we did it because I'll never get that experience again. And it was powerful, but not in a way that I was expecting.

What do you feel was the major issue that led JFK's killers to feel that he had to be so brutally murdered?

As to the question of why they murdered JFK, I think he was going to withdraw. He had signed an executive order to withdraw from Vietnam. I think he was looked upon as a rich kid who didn't deserve the presidency. I think that he was looked upon as someone not deserving to be there and that his father had stolen the election. People that had been in the military, and yes, I'm talking about some of the joint chiefs, feared the country was going to be taken over by communists. The big red dog is loose from these World War II cold warriors. The thing I think about JFK was that once he was in the office, he realized that if we kept going on the path we were going, that chances are that we were going to perish in the flames of war. That it was inevitable, because we had all these weapons and that it was going to happen sooner or later. And he tried to pull back from that. He went from being a cold warrior, to trying to get these weapons under control so that we wouldn't kill each other.

It's quite evident in the peace speech that he gave at American University, where he said we all live on this small planet, we all breathe the same air, we all cherish our children's futures, and we are all mortal. He meant that. And I think that that speech, along with what had happened at the Cuban Missile Crisis, where the military higher-ups felt that he had backed down when he should have gone ahead and went to war over Cuba, combined with their feeling about him not deserving to be there, I think that's the real reason John Kennedy was assassinated. He was looked at as being soft on communism and probably had communist leanings himself, and wasn't man enough to take on the Russians. And of course, we know now that they had nuclear weapons in Cuba at that time, and would have used them had we gone to war. And it's by his intelligence and by luck, that we're alive today.

Some say the Beatles stopped touring because Paul was replaced.
Why do you think that the Beatles stopped touring?

I think the Beatles were tired and wanted to get off the road.

So, is Paul still with us? Where do you cast your vote?

Yes, Paul is still with us. I don't believe for a moment that Paul McCartney died in 1966 in a car wreck, and that the Beatles being this big phenomenon partnered with the government to cover up Paul's death. If they did leave those kinds of clues in their records played backwards or on their album covers, I think they were having a bit of fun with all of us.

I think Paul has talked about it a couple of times. I've seen him in interviews and he does it tongue in cheek. I think he enjoys it a great deal really. But no, I think it's a total hoax. I think people love to believe in it because it's fun and it's titillating, and it's something to delve into.

The problem is that you do have real conspiracies in this world. I do not look at everything as a conspiracy. And because I have a bent toward being cynical and looking at some things and going, "Well, that could be a conspiracy." My own nature is to go, "Well, if there is a conspiracy, then I need proof of it. I don't just bite." But when the evidence is so overwhelming, sometimes you have to say there are conspiracies. If you delve into anything like Project Artichoke, Operation Paperclip, we brought Nazis over here. The government knew about it. We used their skills. They did unheard-of things to people during World War II, experimenting on people. We are capable of great barbarity, but we are capable of great heights as a people and as human beings. We are full of goodness and wonderment and light. And there's a part of us that can sink to the lowest branch. And it's always a fight between the two for people. So, anything I do, I need to be satisfied, at least in my own mind, that there's enough proof to say, "Yes, this was a conspiracy," or "No, this is fanciful." As to whether Paul was killed in an automobile accident and that fact was covered up with the help from the government and the rest of the Beatles, no, I believe that's fanciful. It's fun to delve into. It's fun to think about. But no, I don't believe it. But I also know that we can sometimes live in a world full of nightmares.

John Barbour

John Barbour is known as the Godfather of Reality TV. He created and co-hosted *Real People,* the number one rated show on television at the time. Barbour worked as a stand-up comic, and had numerous other short lived talk shows. He was Frank Sinatra's personal writer for years. He also worked with former New Orleans District Attorney Jim Garrison, and produced two groundbreaking documentaries on the JFK assassination.

Please tell us about yourself?

I'm known as the Godfather of Reality TV having created the 1st reality show and one of the most original and popular in TV history. I am the writer and producer of the 2 definitive docs on the murder of JFK and Jim Garrison's solved, sabotaged investigation, and the author of the best book ever about anyone in Showbiz, with a forward by Don Jeffries, called: *Your Mother's Not A Virgin!'* All and more on: www.johnbarboursworld.com.

When did you first see the Beatles, and how long did it take for you to become a fan?

Their 1st appearance on *Ed Sullivan* on the 1st downbeat. I have every recording, and a wall full of autographed pics and items and 5 huge posters.

Which Beatle is your favorite, and why?

John Lennon. He *is* the Beatles. Not only musically, but intellectually and politically. He has written dozens of things you can quote about life itself. Try to find one from the other 3!!

When did you become aware of the rumors that Paul McCartney was dead?

During the 70's I read a couple of fact-based articles that Paul had been killed in a car crash.

Then again in 2016 I read a couple of articles that said Trump was sent by God!!

Which rumors stand out in your mind, among the 'clues'?
None.

Did you ever play any of your records backwards?

I had no desire to play any of their records, because then it'd sound like Dylan played forward!!

Do you think that the Beatles were behind this as an in-joke? Or did it take them by surprise, as well?

I do not think Lennon would have allowed such a sick joked be imposed on the public. He was as addicted to Truth as music.

Is it true that at an Elvis concert in Vegas during 1969, Ringo Starr was seated next to you and Don Rickles? And Ringo turned to you and remarked to the two of you, "It's a shame that Paul died in that accident."

I was at the '69 Vegas Elvis concert but sat next to my wife.

So, is Paul still with us? Where do you cast your vote?

Paul, indeed well in his solo years but cannot remember one song. Only the money he made. Again, John had the sweetest voice. And in conclusion, instead of worrying about Paul alive or dead, you should be looking into the killers of John. That is a loss to history. Paul alive or dead is just an ok singer with enormous talent, but had he not been a part of the Fab 4, not likely he'd be considered a Fab 1.

Debbie Greenberg

Debbie Greenberg was one of many youngsters in Liverpool who were faithful fans of the Beatles, before they went to America and became iconic. Her father would later own the famous Cavern club where the Fab Four first became well-known in England.

I was born and bred in Liverpool in 1945. The city was dull and depraved after the Second World War with numerous bombsites around the city and beyond. Music played a big part in my life. My father Alf Geoghegan, had a trio called The Ukulele Rhythm Boys and before I was born, would often play on BBC *Workers Playtime* or *Music While you Work*. They also entertained the troops during the war. As a young girl of three or four my dad would play his George Formby ukulele and sing some of his songs to me on a Sunday morning. As I was growing up mum and dad often had friends round to our house of an evening. Mum would play the piano and they would sing all the old ballads of Cole Porter, Irving Berlin and George Gershwin. At the age of twelve I discovered Elvis, then Buddy Holly then Cliff Richard and then Billy Fury who was the UK's answer to Elvis.

At the age of fourteen in 1959 I discovered the Cavern through a friend of mine who was slightly older than me. She took me down to this cellar jazz club in the heart of Liverpool; it was akin to entering a wondrous place. The Cavern had opened on 16th January 1957, it was very atmospheric and the Jazz bands that played were fabulous, The Merseysippi Jazz Band, Acker Bilk, Kenny Ball, Chris Barber and many others. Although I preferred rock 'n' roll, the trad jazz was entertaining. Gradually during 1959 skiffle started to infiltrate and this was great. On 31st October 1959 the Cavern changed hands from Alan Sytner to Ray McFall. Even though Ray was a jazz fanatic, it didn't take him long to realise that what the kids wanted was rock 'n' roll and on 20th November 1959 he introduced the first rock 'n 'roll group to play the Cavern, Rory Storm and The Hurricanes. This was more like it, this is what we wanted. Very soon the Cavern became the 'In' place to go. It was full most nights. On 27th December The Beatles played at Litherland Town Hall on the outskirts of Liverpool. They were billed as direct from Hamburg and by all accounts gave an incendiary performance. They were the talk of the town and when they made their debut performance at the Cavern at a lunchtime session on 9th February 1961, we were expecting to see a German group. When they arrived, it was clear that they were 'Scousers' Liverpudlians and not German at all. The second they bounced on to the stage we were hooked. They were loud, raw, humorous, exciting, intoxicating. Dressed in black T-shirts and trousers and black leather jackets, we couldn't get enough of them. I knew then they were special and was determined to see them every time they played at the Cavern after that, and I did, all 292 times.

I went home to my dad and said, "There is a group on at the Cavern, and you mark my words, they're going to be famous one day." Every time The Beatles played the Cavern was packed. Because the stage was only a foot away from the first row of seats, you could talk to the group and ask for requests and The Beatles always interacted with the audience. It was like a private party every time they played. It was the most magical place on earth, and I couldn't get enough of it. The Cavern had a distinct smell, one which we all carried home with us. It was a combination of Perspiration, condensation, cigarette smoke, disinfectant, hot dogs, soup and the smell of rotting fruit from the fruit exchange opposite the Cavern. It was unbearably hot, but we loved it. The music, the groups and the excitement far outweighed the infamous smell. The Beatles went back to Hamburg on14th March 1961 and out of our lives for over three months. They returned on 14th July and, wow, what a transformation. They were dressed from head to toe in black leather, they were infused with even more vigor and passion than before, they were sexy, raunchy, the music was even louder than before, you could feel your body tremor to the beat. Long before you entered the Cavern you could hear the boom! boom! in Mathew Street, from the group on stage, like a giant heart beating in the cellar below and we couldn't wait to get down those eighteen stone steps to get a piece of the action. I continued to watch The Beatles play and grow in the Cavern right through from Brian Epstein taking them under his wing, the loss of Pete Best and the debut of Ringo on 22nd August at the Cavern, which was filmed by Granada TV, right through to their final appearance at the Cavern on 3rd August 1963. I continued to go to the Cavern after The Beatles left. There were still many good groups in Liverpool, there were more than 300 groups in the early sixties.

Then on 28th February the Cavern closed because Ray McFall had declared bankruptcy. We were all distraught, what on earth were we going to do now. A few weeks later, a life-long friend of my dad's, Joe Davey, told my dad he had the chance to buy the Cavern but couldn't afford it on his own and would he come in with him to buy the Cavern. My dad then came to me and said, "I've got the chance to buy the Cavern, what do you think?" I couldn't believe my own ears, was my dad really thinking of buying the most amazing club on the planet. Even though it was like offering a kid the key to the sweet shop, I had a business head and I said, "Look dad, I've seen the Cavern at its peak, and I think it could happen again." We bought the Cavern and the Prime Minister, Harold Wilson, re-opened it for us on 23rd July 1966. It took us a year to get it back on its feet and then it went from strength to strength. I ran the Club for my dad in 1967 after running and selling our three butchers' shops over a twelve-month period. In 1970 Dad was approached by a friend of his called Harry Waterman who wanted to buy the Cavern. Dad hadn't thought about selling and sat on his offer for a month when Harry approached him again. The Cavern was at its peak and Dad said I suppose it is a good time to sell. At the beginning of November 1970 contracts were signed and exchanged. On17th November Dad received a letter from a firm of solicitors acting on behalf of British Rail, who owned the land that the Cavern stood on. They wanted to put a Bill before Parliament in

January 1971 to build an underground Rail Network under Liverpool city centre and if it was passed it would give them the power to compulsory purchase the Cavern. British Rail wanted the site of the Cavern to build a proposed ventilation shaft for the new network link. Dad passed on the letter to the solicitor to make the buyers aware of the situation. Within a week another letter arrived, saying that if the Cavern owners were prepared to pay the sum of £500.00, British Rail would be prepared to move the site of the proposed shaft further down Mathew Street to Button Street. Dad phoned Harry three times in my presence begging him to pay the money. Harry was a multi-millionaire even in those days and a collector of night clubs. He owned twelve clubs in Liverpool besides the Cavern. After the third time of Dad begging him to pay the £500.00 his reply was apathetic. "Well Alfie, I'll let Roy decide." Roy Adams was his partner in the Cavern and his front man. My dad's pleas for them to save the iconic Cavern which was a shrine and belonged to the world fell on deaf ears. The Cavern was demolished on 3rd June 1973. If only Dad had waited two more weeks to sell the Cavern, we wouldn't have hesitated to pay the £500.00 and the original Cavern would still be standing today. In 2014, I became aware of rumors circulating in Liverpool that the blame for the demolition of the Cavern was being firmly placed at my dad's feet. My dad was no longer able to defend himself as he had passed on some 33 years earlier. I was incensed by the injustice and was determined to set the record straight. My book *Cavern Club-The Inside Story* was published on 24th October 2016 and was launched at the new Cavern Club in Liverpool.

Pete was the quiet Beatle, he was sultry and moody-looking. He didn't want to conform with The Beatles' new hairstyles. Pete had a large fan following; he was a very good-looking guy. Ringo was extremely shy in the early days. His mum Elsie used to come into our butchers shop every Saturday morning, place a ten shilling note on the counter and say, "The usual Deb, our Richie will call in for it later." He would stand in the doorway of the shop, he wouldn't speak. I'd have to say to him "Have you come for your mum's meat, Richie," and he would just nod and take the order of half a leg of lamb and a quarter of boiled ham back across the street to Admiral Grove. Years later we would see Ringo on the drums in Rory Storm and The Hurricanes.

25th October 1968. Paul McCartney made an impromptu visit to the Cavern. My dad was stocking the Top Bar. Dad offered his hand and introduced himself as Alf Geoghegan, the Cavern. Paul shook his hand and said, "Paul McCartney, the Cavern.' He said he had his new girlfriend in the car, and he wanted to show her where it all began. He said he had to deliver a record player to his stepsister Ruth, who lived on the Wirral across the River Mersey, and he would like to come back in about an hour, on one condition, that Dad didn't bring the press in. Dad said, "You've got it." I was at the hairdressers while this was taking place. When I returned, Dad said, "We've had a visitor". Paul McCartney. I thought I'd missed him. Dad said don't worry there's a chance he will come back; you finish stocking the bar and put the champagne on ice, I'm going to buy a camera. Dad went to a photographers' a few blocks away and bought a Yashika camera. He brought the photographer back to the Cavern and he set the apertures on the camera for the lighting in the club. He told Dad not to touch the dials just press the button when you are ready.

We waited, and sure enough Paul returned with Linda, and we closed the door to stop the tourists coming in. We chatted in the Top Bar, there were just five of us, Paul, Linda my dad, me and Paddy Delaney, our head doorman. Dad had contacted him and told him to get down to the Cavern but didn't tell him why. Dad went to pour the champagne when Linda said, "I'll do that, I'm a good bartender." Linda poured the champagne and we reminisced about the early days in the Cavern. Dad asked Paul if we could take some personal photographs. "That's fine," said Paul. Dad went to pick up the camera and Linda said, "I'll do that, I'm a good photographer." Dad's face was a study; I could see he was thinking 'well that's torn it.' We had no idea that Linda was a photographer.

We chatted some more, and Paul told us that he was producing a record for The Ivey's called *Come and Get It*, the theme song for the film, *The Magic Christian*. The Ivey's were like one of the family to us. Dad used to give them regular gigs at the Cavern, then he would bring them home to our house, feed them and give them a bed for the night before they returned to Swansea in South Wales. Paul told Dad he was thinking of changing their name to 'Finger.' Dad said "Oh, I don't like that Paul that's bad." "Badfinger," Paul said. "Thanks Alf," and that's how Badfinger got their name. We chatted a while longer and then we descended the 8-feet-wide staircase down into the Cavern proper where a group that Dad managed called The Curiosity Shoppe where rehearsing on stage. They fell silent when Paul waved to them and said, "Alright lads." What happened next will live with me forever. Paul walked over to an upright piano outside the band room to the left of the stage and started to sing and play *Hey Jude*. It was so surreal as if it was all taking place in slow motion. *Hey Jude* had only been released on 31st August 1968 and aired for the first time on *The David Frost Show* on TV on 8th September so we were probably one of the first public audiences to hear Paul perform it and it was in the original Cavern. I still get goosebumps every time I hear *Hey Jude*, I am instantly transported back to that iconic day in the Cavern. Paul then went through the band room and took his place on the drums and Linda took more photographs. Very soon it was time for them to leave and Dad gave Paul a red T-shirt with the Cavern logo on the front. We waved them off down Mathew Street and then Dad and I dashed down to a photographers' called Jason's in Mathew Street and waited with bated breath in the darkroom for the photographs to be developed. Linda was right; she was a good photographer.

My reaction to Paul's demise was one of disbelief; I didn't accept a word of it. None of them registered with me as I didn't believe any of it. There is no chance of Paul going anywhere. I bet he's got plans of where he's going to be when he's a hundred years old. They could easily fit a stair lift to the stage at Glastonbury. You could try asking Freda, but knowing her as I do, I think it's unlikely.

Ben Ohmart

Ben Ohmart is the founder of BearManor Media, which specializes in publishing books about the world of entertainment.

Please tell us about yourself, and what you are working on.

I'm Ben Ohmart, working on a musical version of Paul Frees' *The Beatniks*, in between handling bearmanormedia.com daily. Books take up a Lot of my time, so it's taken me a decade to finish this musical!

When did you first see the Beatles, and how long did it take for you to become a fan?

Never SAW them, but when I went away to junior college and left TV watching behind, I became more engrossed in music, buying all the cassette tapes I could find in stores. Grabbed that blue-covered Beatles' greatest hits because I recognized some of the names of the songs. But when I started to play the tape - wow! I'd heard every song before! Well, except for the Indian music. :) But the Beatles is like air - everywhere you go, it's there. They are TUNEFUL, unlike today when it's "the singer, not the song," and man, I do dig songs you can whistle.

Which Beatle became your favorite, and why did that member appeal to you?

Has to be Paul because he's an engine. The more I read about Lennon, the more I'm pretty sure I wouldn't like him if I met him. But that doesn't stop me from buying every massive set he or Paul or George put out. Okay. I don't have any Ringo CDs in the house - sorry!

When did you become aware of the rumors that Paul McCartney was replaced by Billy Shears?

That'll have to be when I read Your book.

Which 'clues' from the record covers stand out the most in your mind?

I'm afraid the covers don't speak to me, except *Pepper* and *We're Only in It for the Money* which probably beats the Beatles' cover for greatness because no Beatle is wearing a dress.

Did you play any of your vinyl records backwards looking for 'messages'?

Haven't owned a record player since the 80s, man! Strictly a CD and sometimes streaming person. But I get all the CDs of the music I like so that no one can delete them from my life if they feel like it.

The songs held many 'clues' (even played forward), which ones resonated to you?

Oh dear, maybe you'll have to delete my responses because I've got NO input on this subject for ya, sorry!

When the Beatles stopped touring, some say it was because Paul was no longer with us. Why do you think the group stopped touring?

I don't think there's any truth to Paul being someone else. He looks/acts too much like himself. It's fun to think it, like UFOs and it mattering what political party's in charge, but I don't see any Reason to. But I look forward to you convincing me!

Paul played many songs from the Beatle studio years live for the first time. What do you think of that, and his legacy as a solo artist?

He's GREAT. Best songwriter ever. Beats the pants off Dylan, because he can sing. It's just too bad the world now cares more about How you sing than what you sing, and that you can't be old and have a hit. But. The man had a lot of hits, he's still a Gentleman, and he'll Never be forgotten, long after all the alphabet group rappers are.

So, is Paul still with us? Where do you cast your vote?
Here!

Cindy Sheehan

Cindy Sheehan is an international peace activist who rose to national prominence following the death of her son Casey in Iraq during the George W. Bush administration.

Please tell us about yourself, and any projects you are working on.
I am a peace and social justice activist; author, podcaster, and video show host. *Cindy Sheehan's Soapbox Newsletter and Substack.*

When do you first recall becoming aware of the Beatles, and how long did it take for you to become a fan?
My mother was quite a rocker, so she introduced us kids to the Beatles. When they'd be on *The Ed Sullivan Show*, she'd call us into the house.

Did you have a favorite Beatle, and why did they stand out to you?
Paul and Ringo were my favorites and John and George were my sisters'. I like Paul because I thought he was so cute and I liked Ringo because he was the drummer---I think he was my first drummer I had a crush on.

What did you think of John Lennon, and his stance against the Vietnam War?
I wasn't too aware of it back during the Vietnam War because I wasn't very old, but as an adult I appreciate it. I used to have a shirt with John Lennon's face on a peace sign, and Yoko saw a picture of

me wearing it, so we became friends and she became a patron of my work. Her close associate told me John's peace work was heavily influenced by Yoko.

When did you first hear of the rumors that Paul was replaced in the band?

I never heard those rumors, but I heard he was dead because of the cover of *Abbey Road* where he was out of step. And then there were the incidences of the back-masking on the *White Album.* "Turn me on dead man" and "Paul is Dead," etc.

Did you ever play your vinyl records backwards looking for 'clues'?

Yes. Of course, I did. Poor kids who can't do that anymore.

Which 'clues' from the record album covers stand out to you?

I think I answered that.

Some say that the Beatles stopped touring because Paul had been replaced. Why do you think that the Beatles stopped touring?

I think they stopped touring because they got tired of it, Yoko's influence on John took them away; and I think they wanted to retire on top.

On a more serious note, what do you think John Lennon would think about the current situation in the Ukraine?

I am not sure where John would be. I see a lot of his contemporary (or a little later) singers/songwriters supporting "Ukraine" and all of the fascist Covid/vaccine mandates. I hope he'd still be a peace-nik, but it's hard to say. I haven't heard Yoko's take on Ukraine.

So, is Paul still with us? Where do you cast your vote?

If Paul's not still with us, is that a clone that was in Wings and still alive? I read that Paul McCartney has denied he's dead. LOL.

Diane Renay

Diane Renay is a singer who is probably best remembered for her 1963 Top Ten single *Navy Blue*. The follow-up single, considered a "sequel" of sorts, *Kiss Me Sailor,* was also a Top 40 hit the following year.

Please tell us all about yourself, and your long and fascinating career.

I am recording artist Diane Renay who had the Billboard top ten hit *Navy Blue*. The Beatles had the top 3 songs on the chart when I was up there with them! I currently have 2 albums you can purchase or download at Amazon, iTunes and other music sites. The names of the albums are as follows....*Navy Blue 25 Super Tracks*. This album has all of the songs that were on the original *Navy Blue* album plus many other songs that were never released! The second Album is titled...*Diane Renay Sings "Some Things Old & Some Things New."* It is a double CD with new songs that that I recorded in the1980's which were never released and it has the Dance Version I recorded of *Navy Blue* that was also never released! And, I have a Facebook with many interesting photos of me with some of the artists that I performed with...this includes the Rolling Stones, the Supremes and many other great artists that I worked with. Also, I have some of my recordings that many people have never heard on my Facebook that you can listen too for your enjoyment.

How were you discovered, and when did you sign your first recording contract?

I started recording when I was only 16 years old. I met my first record producer Pete De Angelis who produced Bobby Rydell, Al Martino etc. through a customer of my father who had a jewelry store in Philadelphia. The customer was Pete's cousin and he arranged for me to meet Pete and sing for him. My parents drove me to Pete De Angelis's home in New Jersey and he played his piano while I sang a couple of standard songs for him. When I finished Peter turned to my parents and told them he can get me a recording contract with ATCO records which was a subsidiary of Atlantic Records. Pete produced my first single which was the standard song *Little White Lies*. It got air play enough for ATCO to give me one more session according to my contract. For that session they called in record producer Bob Crewe who was the producer and writer of the songs that the Four Seasons had big hits on... *Sherry*, *Walk Like a Man* and *Big Girls Don't Cry* at the time I met Bob Crewe. He produced my second release that he co wrote *Tender*. Well the song hit charts here and there but not enough for ATCO to pick up my contract so they let me go. That was the best thing that happened to me because Bob Crewe asked my father if he could take me on as one of his own artists to produce records for me and be my manager! Well the rest is history....the next session that Bob produced and co-wrote the song I sang was *Navy Blue!* Actually *Navy Blue* was the B-Side of the single release song *Unbelievable Guy* that Bob also wrote for me. I was still in high school when all of this was happening. I came home from school one day and the phone rang and it was Bob Crewe. He said to me, "Sit down I have something to tell you," "you have a hit record and you will never guess which song it is....." *Navy Blue*!!! The B-Side of the record!

How did you first learn about the Beatles?

My talent agency was William Morris Talent Agency in New York. Well I was up in their offices to see my personal agent and all was a buzz about the "BEATLES" coming to the US! The whole agency was talking about them before they even arrived here. That's how I heard about them. Before the Beatles landed in the US my William Morris Talent Agent asked me if I wanted to go on tour with the Beatles as their opening act! I was their first choice. However, my agent also warned me that if I go the kids will be screaming throughout my entire act! He said if it would bother me I might want to back out from the offer. It would have bothered me if I was performing and no one was listening because they were screaming "We Want The Beatles!" So I decided not to go on tour with the Beatles. Now I wish I had gone on tour with them, to know them would have been an honor.

Did you have a favorite Beatle, and why?

I loved all of the Beatles I did not have a favorite one. Their songs were amazing!

Do you know what the Beatles thought of Navy Blue *or your other music?*

My song was on the Top Ten Billboard list with the Beatles having the first three songs. I imagine they must have heard *Navy Blue* played on the radio as much as their own hits at the time. I have no idea what they thought about my song.

When did you first hear about the "Paul is Dead" rumors?

I never heard about the rumor that Paul was dead until my second marriage that was in 1992. My second husband Chris Eagan, who is a professional musician/inventor/author, just loved the Beatles and he told me about the song regarding that Paul was dead! LOL!!

Do you still listen to the Beatles? To any of their solo works?

My husband Chris Eagan and I watch the Beatles on YouTube all the time! We are amazed at how they were so young and wrote such profound lyrics to their songs. They were real composers of some of the best songs ever written!

So where do you come down - is Paul still with us?

Paul is very much alive!!!! And so is Ringo!!! It's just a shame that John never lived his life to create more great songs, he was the best! Also, it is sad that George left us much too soon. On his own he was a great artist all by himself!

Ellen Dubin

Tell us about yourself. Please promote any work, links, etc. that you like?

I am a lover of all things entertainment! I am a stage, film, television and voiceover actress. I started my career in ballet because my parents put me in dance class as I was a shy child and had flat feet. Little did I know, during each of the end of year recitals, that the performance bug would take over! I loved the response of a live audience and would always do an extra arm wave to move an audience or instinctively wait for a beat to get a laugh. I was hooked! I ended up doing a lot of stage from farce to drama to Shakespeare to musicals. I studied piano, singing and all forms of dance and improvisation. I was always striving to learn more.

Flash forward, even though at the time I didn't watch a lot of Sci-fi/fantasy type of TV shows, I ended up doing a lot of Sci-fi shows as an actress. This wild and and crazy show called **Lexx** put me on the map in that genre. The fan base is loyal and wonderful in the science-fiction world. And I ended up going to various conventions and meeting these incredibly loyal followers to which I am so grateful.

Some other career highlights include being in one of the biggest cult comedies of all time *Napoleon Dynamite* and starring in a wonderful supernatural drama called *The Collector* for which I was nominated a *Gemini* for Best Dramatic Actress.

In the last 10 years, I have discovered the love of voiceover work. How wonderful to know that I can voice all ages, all different kinds of creatures, humans, robots. I can be a lizard, a beast, a zombie mother, an Orc. I can be a queen or pilot. I can be anything through just the sheer power of my voice.

Some of my favorite credits are the Bene Gesserit Ancestors in the multi-Oscar Winning *Dune*, Captain Phasma in the Emmy-nominated *Star Wars Resistance* and all the *Lego Star Wars* television specials! I am proud to be the narrator of the *60th anniversary of Disneyland* opposite Walt Disney and all *World of Colors* at California Adventureland. I absolutely love doing video games as an actress including the popular titles of *Fallout 4* (BTVA winner), Skyrim, *Elder Scrolls, Star Wars Uprising, World of Warcraft* and *Guild Wars 2*.

When I am not working, I love good food, listening to music and watching all kinds of films and TV shows. I passionately love teaching video game voiceover acting!

You can check me out:

ellendubin.com
Instagram @ EllenDubinActor
Facebook Fan Page: Ellen Dubin Actor
Streamily: Ellen Dubin

When did you first discover the Beatles?

My parents played all kinds of music when I was growing up. I was very fortunate to have a wide range of music to listen to. And they played a lot of Beatles. I used to dance around the living room to their incredible music. And we would sing *Imagine* and *Eleanor Rigby*. I know, not the most cheerful tunes. But, then we would switch to *Yellow Submarine*! A family concert.

One of my wedding songs was *Something*! We both loved that song. A medley of Beatles music is always standing by on the playlist!

Did you have a favorite Beatle? If so, why?

Oh this is a tough one! I remember growing up that all the girls said that Paul McCartney was the cute one – John Lennon was the eclectic one – Ringo Starr was the neglected one – and George Harrison was the quiet one. I can't pick.

But George Harrison did write two of my favorite Beatles' songs: *Something* and *While My Guitar Gently Weeps*! They get to my very soul!

Did you ever see the Beatles live in concert?

Never. I wish. A bit before my time.

How did you first hear the "Paul is Dead" rumors?

I was late to the party on this one. And then a few friends started talking about it and I started to do a little bit of research into this intriguing rumor! It became one of the biggest conspiracy stories in the music industry. I heard there were courses offered about this in colleges. It became such a phenomenon!

What "clues" to the rumor do you remember?

I remember hearing the rumor of Paul driving away from Abbey Road after a supposed argument with his band mates and saying that he blew his mind out on in a car. And then the other "theory" was that they said it was a car crash where he was decapitated. And that the rest of the members of the Beatles kept it a secret until they could replace him with an exact doppelgänger. And that the "fake" Paul, wrote *Hey Jude* and *Blackbird.* Wow, what a talent!

And this one was a fascinating one – that the word *Walrus* was a Greek code for "corpse" but it's apparently a Scandinavian word.

I also remember hearing that one album back cover, *Sgt Pepper*, had all the members of the band facing front except Paul!! So that could have been a clue to the "fake" Paul.

And of course the records playing backwards with symbols of death etc. The "I buried Paul" lyric that John recites in *Strawberry Fields Forever* also contributed to the death gossip. It certainly helped the sales of their albums. There were clubs dedicated to finding these death-like lyrics.

And there was Paul walking across Abbey Road *barefoot* as a symbol of his "death".

Did you ever play your records backwards?

Nope!

Did Napoleon Dynamite like the Beatles? How about Uncle Rico?

If Napoleon Dynamite could dance to their music in moon boots, of course! And I would think that he would probably sit in his basement playing those records endlessly backwards and sharing his findings with his brother Kip and best friend Pedro. I think it would blow his mind!

I can just hear him saying: "Sweet"!

Maybe, Uncle Rico could have played Beatles music in his van while he's selling his Tupperware! I think the ladies would have liked that and he would have sold a lot of lids! LOL!

Do you still listen to the Beatles' music?

I certainly do! My mother and I still listen to them. Their music is timeless! Never gets old! I think of John's horrible death and miss his whole vibe.

Every time I went to Las Vegas, I had to see Cirque du Soleil's amazing show *LUV* to the Beatles' music - A perfect combination of classic Beatles music and Cirque du Soleil's fascinating spin on their music!

How about their solo work?

I still love their old work the best when they were together as a group. But yes, I do follow their work. I really want to see Ringo Starr - he's been touring. And of course Paul has had a solo career for a long time. And, I think his recent tour just ended. Keeping a look out for the next one!

So how do you vote? Is Paul McCartney still with us?

Oh, he's definitely alive and well! And making fabulous music!

Should we try for immortality? And buck the system! 😆 !

Unless, he is sitting with James Dean, Elvis and Marilyn Monroe?

Monte A. Melnick

Monte Melnick's long career in music was highlighted by his position as road manager for the Ramones.

Will you please tell us about yourself, and what you are up to?

Over the remarkable twenty-two-year career of the Ramones, the seminal punk rock band, Monte A. Melnick saw it all. Monte was with the band from the very early CBGB dates to the final show in 1996, touring the world in over 2,200 shows, working his way up to be their Tour Manager. The Ramones are Rock 'n' Roll Hall of Famers, Grammy and MTVs Lifetime Achievement Award winners and inducted into The Library of Congress' National Recording Registry. Monte is now working as the In House Manager at the Queens Theatre in the Park, the premier performing arts center in Queens New York. He also served as the Audio Visual Supervisor at the New York Hall of Science for over 16½ years. In the early 70's as a bass player he was a signed artist with the rock band 'Thirty Days Out', with two albums on Reprise/Warner Brothers Records. Monte has participated in numerous podcasts and celebrity panels. He is the author of the book, *On The Road with the Ramones*, published in seven languages, currently available on Amazon.com worldwide in a new BONUS EDITION.

When did you first become aware of the Beatles, and how long did it take before you became a fan?

From the very first record, I always liked the Beatles.

Did any of the Beatles become your favorite, and what made them stand out to you?

Always liked John Lennon the best. His songwriting and later solo work hit a special note with me.

Did the Beatles have anything to do with the Ramones choosing their name?

Yes they did. Dee Dee saw that Paul McCartney was checking himself into hotels as Paul Ramon, so he said to the band let's name ourselves Ramones and take the last name.

Can you please relate one of the best stories from the world of rock and roll? I speak of the Ramones at a Texas gas station.

This was early on. We were driving through rural Texas, driving five or six hours, and we pulled into a gas station to get some gas, and there was a little store there, too, so they all pile out of the van, looking like zombies. They were staggering around because they had been in the van for hours. So they're in the store looking at stuff, and I come in to pay for the gas and the lady says, "It's sure nice of you to take care of these retarded boys." I said, "Yes ma'am, that's my job."

When did you first hear the rumors that Paul McCartney may have been replaced by a double?

Not sure.

Did you ever play your vinyl records backwards?

No.

Some think that the Beatles stopped touring because Paul was replaced by Billy Shears. Why do you suspect that the Beatles stopped touring?

Exhaustion, poor venue sound quality and amp; concerns over their personal safety and wellbeing. Other factors – such as the death of their manager Brian Epstein and a desire for improved musical development – also contributed to the decision.

Did the Ramones playing fast sets have anything to do with the influence of the Beatles?

No.

So, is Paul still with us? Where do you cast your vote?

Yes, he still is with us.

Richie Furay

Richie Furay is a singer-songwriter and member of the Rock and Roll Hall of Fame. He founded the iconic band Buffalo Springfield with Stephen Stills and Neil Young, as well as the group Poco with Randy Meisner and Jim Messina. He also was part of the successful Souther Hillman Furay Band, along with J.D. Souther and Chris Hillman, formerly of the Byrds.

Please tell us about yourself, and what you're up to. Has the Lord given you a higher calling these days?

Like everyone else I've been waiting for the Covid crisis to settle down. Just before it shut things down I'd recorded an album of country covers that had left their mark on me over the years. It was released in July on BMG. So I've been doing a lot of interviews and stuff that goes along with making recordings today. I've also been working on a documentary (*Through It All*).

We have Cameron Crowe doing the narration and it's the story of my life that David Stone (my manager) and Denny Klein (his partner) felt was worthy of production. As for as the "higher calling" – I still remain a servant of the LORD Jesus Christ – it's as high on that ladder as one can get.

When did you first see the Beatles, and how long did it take for you to become a fan?

Pretty much like everyone else it was on *The Ed Sullivan Show* – that was my first visual. Of course their music was resonating with me even though folk music was still my focus at the time. I would say I was a fan of their early music – they were a phenomena; they were doing something new but it was very accessible; with all the radio airplay, it made it easy to become a fan. I can't remember or say for sure if it was gradual or not, all I remember was – these guys were pretty cool. Their songs had great melodies and in the beginning the lyrics were pretty straightforward – everything was right out front, you knew what they were talking.

Did the Beatles have an effect on your own music, and in what way?

When Stephen Stills and I started Buffalo Springfield we sat around learning all the songs Stephen had written that would be on the first album. The dynamics of John and Paul singing was something that certainly influenced us and, you might say we modeled some of our vocal arrangements from them – singing in unison, in particular. That seemed to be something new and we did that on several songs on our first record.

Did you have a favorite Beatle, and why did that one stand out to you?

John, I don't know exactly why; if you were to ask people who were looking on at the time of the early Springfield they'd probably make the comparison of me with (George – the guy in the middle) or Paul – he was the smoother singer, but John is the one I identified with.

When did you learn about the rumors of Paul being replaced by Billy Shears? What did you make of that?

I don't remember that at all – (maybe it was when I pretty much dropped out of music for awhile).

Did you ever play your vinyl records backwards?

Not that I recall. I know we played tape in the studio backwards or upside down but I never personally played any vinyl "backwards".

Which clues from the record covers resonated with you?

I guess I wasn't paying attention – no clues.

Some say the Beatles stopped touring because Paul was replaced. Why do you think that the Beatles stopped touring?

Like almost every other "successful" band in that era (except for the Stones, of course) – things happen when you get creative people together. It's almost how some people find themselves in a marriage relationship. When it's just getting started, it's all smiles and "yeah, yeah, yeah – yeah" – we'll be in love forever; but as time goes on it can become tedious, you have to work at, you have to learn give and take … and things change; some don't want to give as much as the others and, one day – it all falls apart. (It didn't happen overnight; it may seem that way but … … … !)

Many songs from the studio years were never played live by the Beatles. Paul has played these songs, and people at concerts love them. What do you think about this part of Paul's legacy?

I think it's cool that he goes back and revisits some material – in a way it says, "yeah, we had some fun and then some!"

So, is Paul still with us? Where do you cast your vote?

Still with us; still out there filling the stadiums!

Jim Berkenstadt

Jim Berkenstadt is an author, record producer, and historical entertainment consultant, popularly known as "the Rock and Roll Detective."

Please tell us how the Rock and Roll Detective came into being?

Well, I guess it is when I started collecting records as far back as 1964. *Meet the Beatles* was my first LP. *I Want to Hold Your Hand* was my first 45 rpm single. I wanted to know everything about the music I loved. Who produced it? Who wrote the song? How did they choose the A-side and B-side? Who played what instruments? Could I pick out who was singing which harmony part? As time went on, I wanted to find out about the musicians who influenced The Beatles and also learn more about the bands that were contemporaries of The Beatles. At age 10, I decided I wanted to work for The Beatles. Although I grew up and became a lawyer, I never let go of that dream. In the early 90s I teamed up with Belmo to write *Black Market Beatles: The Story Behind Their Lost Recordings*. Then, when my friend Butch Vig produced a little band in the 90s named Nirvana, I wrote a book with Charles Cross (*Nevermind Nirvana*) about the behind the scenes making of the *Nevermind* album. By 1998, I was asked by George Harrison to locate some lost recordings of his. He later recommended me to The Beatles' company Apple and I began working for Neil Aspinall, Paul, George, later Olivia, Yoko and Ringo. Some dreams do come true, if you keep visualizing your dream job and work towards it. My latest book in 2022 is called *Mysteries in the Music: Case Closed*, a series of different mysteries in Rock and Roll that no one had ever solved. In the 90s I realized that the research and consulting I did, made me a Rock And Roll Detective®. Neil Aspinall once joked with me about being a music detective. So, I trademarked the name and it became my brand. Best job in the world!

You have done research for an impressive lot of people, and have such wonderful books. Please clue us in about all of that, will you?

For George Harrison, I did a lot of research into alternate takes, demos, and outtakes from the *All Things Must Pass* album which he re-mastered at the end of his life. And again I worked with Dhani Harrison on the same album for the new, remixed Uber Box Set of ATMP. I spent a lot of time consulting on George Harrison's *Dark Horse Years* box set with Olivia Harrison, as well as a new version of *Living in the Material World*, and the *Traveling Wilburys box set*. One of my biggest thrills was when Olivia Harrison called me and asked me to be the Historical Consultant to Martin Scorsese for the Harrison biopic, *George Harrison: Living in the Material World.* I have served as a historical consultant to Butch Vig, the band Garbage, and as a rock expert on two series' at the REELZ channel; a Hulu documentary on The Bealtes; and recently a heavy metal documentary for Paramount+. For The Beatles, I worked on the *Help!* Box Set, the audio for the Cirque du Soleil Love show, the *Eight Days a Week* documentary and the *Get Back* Documentary on Disney+.

When did you first become aware of the Beatles, and how long did it take for you to be hooked?

I first became aware of The Beatles about a week before they appeared on *The Ed Sullivan Show* in February, 1964. My mom showed me a photograph on the front page of the *Chicago Tribune* with 4 guys having a pillow fight. It looked funny, so I thought they were the next Laurel and Hardy or Marx Brothers. Boy, was I surprised when they came on the show and were playing loud rock and roll that I instantly loved. I was hooked for life on that night.

At what point in time did you first hear about the "Paul is Dead" rumors, and how did you learn about that?

I first heard about the "Paul is Dead" rumors in the fall of 1969 when they first surfaced. I think I heard it on the nightly news. Then somewhere I saw a list of the clues on albums and covers that were supposed to prove The Beatles were trying to tell all of us that Paul had died. Our newspaper had a story about the rumor starting with a DJ in Michigan who had read a story about it in a college newspaper.

What caused the Beatles to stop touring, and how did that play into the fervor of the rumors?

I don't think any outside force stopped The Beatles from touring. It seems that collectively the group had grown weary of playing a lot of the same songs over and over to crowds of screaming kids, who could barely hear them. Ringo couldn't even hear the rest of the band from his drum riser. The band and their music had matured and there was really no way to play some of the new material live, due to the overdubs and other instrumentation that could not be reproduced technologically in those days. One can imagine that with The Beatles out of the public eye for a couple of years, that any and all rumors could start up about the group, from a pre-mature breakup, to buying and moving to a private island in Greece (which they did consider), to the "Paul is Dead" rumor. Paul had moved up to a farm in Scotland for some peace and quiet with his family. So being out of the London limelight and clubs made Paul the most likely person subject to a rumor. Keep in mind that in those days, so many fans were starting to experiment with marijuana, LSD and other drugs. These hallucinogenic drugs could have fueled the imaginations of the college kids who wrote the first article about Paul being dead. Recall that Charles Manson's acid fueled listening sessions to The Beatles' *White Album* caused him to believe the group was talking to him about a race war, from listening to *Helter Skelter* and *Piggies*.

You are a detective, and the Sgt. Pepper *album is filled with clues. In your own words, please tell us about some of them?*

They are plain to see! □ Seriously, these clues have been discussed for decades. I am not going to rehash.

We also have a bunch of clues on Abbey Road. *Would you describe them for us, using your keen detective's eye?*

They are plain to see! □ Seriously, these clues have been discussed for decades. I am not going to rehash.

Did the rumors about Paul increase record sales, as it received so much publicity?

I believe that the sales of *Abbey Road* were indeed enhanced by the "Paul is Dead" rumor. Whenever an artist in any creative medium dies, their art usually becomes in higher demand.

Is there any chance that the Beatles did this as a lark, in your estimation?

They did not do this as a joke. There were so many people doing hallucinogenic drugs in the 60s and The Beatles were the top artists of the century, so it is not surprising that college students came up with this silly concept, and then word spread in a pre-viral world.

If Billy Shears really took Paul's place, could he have been a Wilbury?

No. Because of the following reasons: 1. Billy was a fictional character. 2. He didn't replace Paul, and 3. Since George clearly would not have, and did not choose, the living Paul McCartney to be in the Wilburys, he sure as hell would not have selected a Paul stand-in. If you read my book, *Mysteries in the Music: Case Closed*, you will see that the origination of the Traveling Wilburys and the way the group was formed and shared songwriting royalties, was clearly an outgrowth of George's dissatisfaction with Paul and John keeping all of the their publishing money, even when George contributed to their songs lyrically and musically.

So, is Paul still with us? Where do you cast your vote? :)

Yes. Paul is still with us. Linda Eastman did not suddenly go along with a conspiracy and agree to sleep with a stranger named "Billy Shears" after Paul's alleged death. Additionally, the death of a Beatle in the late 1960s could not have been covered up by the police, the band's management, the group, and/or the media. Someone would have leaked it. Also, international Beatles autograph expert Frank Caiazzo, has reviewed the autographs of Paul, both before "he blew his mind out in a car" and after. He has concluded that the autographs from "before" and "after" (including ones Paul wrote on legal agreements) are all written by the one and only Paul McCartney. Case Closed.

Nichole Michael

Nichole Michael is a communications and public relations specialist who markets authors and artists.

Please tell us about yourself, and what you're working on.

I've worked in the communications field for over two decades, and am currently in my seventh year running 910 Public Relations, an independent company that specializes in marketing for authors and artists in the Beatles/music genre. It may sound niche – and it is – but we're quite busy all the time! I also co-own media company Wonderwall with author Kenneth Womack, where we share production and promotional duties. It's all been quite a blessing and I'm grateful every day to be able to work in an industry I love.

When did you first see the Beatles, and what impression did they have on you? How long did it take until you became a fan?

I'm a "second generation" fan, as they say – I first heard the Beatles as a child in the '80s, when my parents would play the oldies/classic rock station in the car. Whenever I'd hear a song I really liked, I would ask them who sang it – and the answer was almost always the Beatles. As a pre-teen, I discovered my uncle's record collection of remastered Beatles vinyls, and asked him to record them onto cassette tapes for me so I could listen. He did, and it was all over – I was completely hooked on the Beatles and soon knew every word to every song on every album.

Do you have a favorite Beatle, and what about them appeals to you?

Ringo Starr. All day, every day. He's uniquely talented, and yet unassuming and effortlessly cool. I just adore him – always have.

When did you first hear rumors that Paul may have died, and been replaced in the Beatles?

I remember being about eight years old and somehow coming into possession of a tape where a man was telling the story of the rumor and all the various clues. It creeped me out at the time, and I didn't even really know what he was talking about!

Did you ever play any of your vinyl records backwards looking for clues?

No, by the time I had vinyls of my own, I'd already heard the backwards recordings through other sources. So I didn't want to risk ruining my own collection.

Some of the songs also are said to have clues in them. Do any stand out to you?

"The walrus was Paul" line in *Glass Onion* always stuck with me. I sometimes still use it in everyday conversation!

The album covers had 'clues' on them. Which ones stand out in your mind?

The flowers on the cover of *Sgt. Pepper* that supposedly spell out "Be at Leso" and "Paul?" were always interesting to me. Also, the "skull" in the shadow on the wall next to the lady walking in the blue dress, on the back of *Abbey Road.*

Some say the Beatles stopped touring because Paul was gone. Why do you think that the Beatles stopped touring?

There were a number of reasons, but I believe they stopped touring because it had become too dangerous and exhausting, in addition to struggling to keep a high level of sound quality with all the crowd noise. Leaving the tour life also afforded the band time to work on other creative pursuits in the studio.

What do you think of Paul's solo career, and concerts? He brought some songs from the studio years to the stage for the first time, what do you think of that?

I've seen Paul in concert seven times and loved every minute of every show. I've always been a big fan of Wings and some of his other solo work as well, and am grateful to hear any of it live. I remember *Temporary Secretary* being a fun treat in more recent years!

So, is Paul still with us? Where do you cast your vote?

He is. To paraphrase Apple's press release about the Beatles' "state of the union" in April 1970, Paul is "alive and well…and the beat goes on."

Victoria Jackson

Victoria Jackson is an actress and comedienne who was a cast member on *Saturday Night Live* from 1986-1992. She also starred in films like *Family Business, The Couch Trip, UHF,* and *Casual Sex.*

Please tell us all about yourself

Born in 1959, Victoria Jackson grew up in a Bible-believing, piano-playing, TV-free home in Miami. Her father coached gymnastics so she competed from age 5-18. Her gymnastic skill led to a college scholarship to Furman University, where she was cast in her first play and got the acting bug. When Johnny Crawford (*The Rifleman*) met her at a Birmingham summer stock production, he bought her a one-way ticket to Hollywood to be in his night club act. For two years, she held odd jobs in the showbiz capital — as a cigarette girl, waitress, and typist — until Johnny Carson noticed her stand-up routine and put her on *The Tonight Show...* twenty times. After that, she starred in many movies and TV shows, most notably six seasons on *Saturday Night Live.*

Jackson was reunited with and married her high school sweetheart, helicopter pilot Paul Wessel in 1992 and when he retired in 2013 from the Miami Dade Police Dept. they moved to Nashville to be near their daughters and grandchildren. Jackson still appears in occasional films, does stand-up comedy, sings her original ukulele songs around town and most recently was nominated for Best Supporting Actress by the International Christian Film Festival for her role as Alma in *Lost Heart* (2021). Jackson authored *Is My Bow Too Big?* published by White Hall in 2012 about how she got on TV, and in 2017 she wrote *Lavender Hair,* published by Broadstreet, about her breast cancer journey and recovery. In 2021 Jackson got her Master's in Film from Lipscomb University and wrote her first screenplay that she is shopping around, "Jane Blond Saves the World, (One Mistake at a Time)". She just finished a short film for the 168 Film Festival and for the rest of 2022, Victoria is doing a stand-up comedy tour; WI, NE, WA, IN, KY, and FL.

How did you first hear about the Beatles?

I first heard about The Beatles when I was five years old at Camp Ocala in FL. My dad was the Gymnastics Coach at a Jewish Camp. We were Baptists and not supposed to dance or listen to rock and roll. I heard my parents disagreeing about whether I could dance with a five-year-old boy at the Big End of Summer Dance. The song that was playing was *I Want to Hold Your Hand*. Mom let me dance. I was wearing a pink dress and felt kind of naughty. I shyly did the twist with the boy. I liked The Beatles songs and harmonies. The melodies were unpredictable. A new sound. Something about the music seemed sexual. I think that drugs, and "the pill," in the 60's influenced the music of that era.

Did you have a favorite Beatle? If so, why?

Favorite Beatle? Well...I'm not a fan of Lennon because he wrote *Imagine* and though the music is lovely, the lyrics are nihilistic. Paul seems to be the happiest Beatle, and family-oriented.

Have you ever met any of the Beatles, on Saturday Night Live *or elsewhere?*

I have never met a Beatle. I did meet Sting though, and Kurt Cobain, and Weird Al.

When did you first hear about the "Paul is Dead" rumors?

"Paul is Dead" rumor. I heard about it briefly when I was a teenager, I think.

Do you remember what clues to this rumor caught your attention?

I was in a Christian high school where we weren't allowed to listen to rock and roll, so I wasn't personally invested in the death rumor or the hype of the Beatles.

Did you ever play your vinyl records backwards?

How do you play a record backwards?!

Do you still listen to Beatles records? To any of their solo efforts?

I don't listen to Beatles records. I recently listened to Joni Mitchell's *Both Sides Now*, and Brandi Carlisle's *The Story*. I play Christian worship music to restore my soul and for massages I play New Age. Listening to my favorites, The Carpenters, *The Best of Bread*, Billy Joel and Carly Simon makes me too nostalgic. I go through phases. One year in the 90's, I listened to The Mamas and The Papas every day. Sometimes classical. It makes me feel smart and clean.

What was your most memorable moment working on Saturday Night Live?

My most memorable moment while working at *SNL* was the Steve Martin/Sting show in 1987 where I sang my original song, *I Am Not a Bimbo* on the Update Desk.

So how do you cast your vote- is Paul still with us?

I think Paul McCartney is still alive and he looks great. And, he still looks happy!

Mitch Weissman

Mitch Weissman is a musician who's worked with many big artists, but is probably best known for playing Paul on Broadway in *Beatlemania.*

Please tell us about yourself, and your work.

My name is Mitch Weissman. Actor, musician, writer. Known for my Broadway role as Paul in *Beatlemania* back in the day. Wrote and played on a variety of artists albums over the years. Notably, KISS, Billy Squier. Many more.

Talking about Paul McCartney doubles who were musical, well you are the first one that comes to mind. How did you come to star in Beatlemania on Broadway?

I auditioned for an unknown production back in 1976. "Wanted: singers, musicians, Beatle look-alikes for unique opportunity." The ad was in *Rolling Stone* and on bulletin boards in music stores on Long Island.

What music influenced you, and when did you first pick up an instrument?

I was raised and surrounded by music in my early years. My parents loved classical, jazz and Broadway shows. Lots of albums in the house. Spent a lot of nights listening to Rimsky-Korsakov, Stravinsky, Tchaikovsky, Mussorgsky and more. Could be where my "heavy" came from. And like most kids, the radio. Four Tops, Supremes, Chuck Berry, Dave Clark Five, Stones, Kinks...and of course the Beatles.

When you first took the stage at the Wintergarden, clamor for a Beatles reunion was high. What was it like for you before these audiences, and in the New York nightlife?

It was a pretty heady experience. Toast of the town, etc. Performing in front of new live audiences every night, some of the best music ever. It was magical. Some of the matinee shows with screaming kids drowning you out gave a glimpse as to what the Beatles must have experienced at some of their shows. And the nightlife was filled with meeting some of my own idols from the arts, theater and the musical arenas of the day.

Did you ever meet any of the Beatles, or did any of them see the show?

There have been stories to that affect. John Lennon told me his 16-year-old son had seen it. Paul is rumored to have seen it with Linda, one of the later stripped-down productions. Their lawyers saw it many times! LOL!

When did you first hear of the Paul is Dead rumors, and what did you make of them?

High school. Read the news reports. Had an album discussing the subject that was very cool if inaccurate. Great stories and clues. Believable in fact.

Which clues from the album covers and in the songs stand out to you?

Well, there were lots of audio clues. "Turn me on, Deadman" from *Revolution #9*. "I buried Paul" from the *Strawberry Fields* fade out. Visually, "28 IF" from the *Abbey Road* cover. Others.

You also sang on Gene Simmons solo record, with Beatlemania cast member Joe Pecorino, as John & Paul did not sign onto the project. What was that like for you? Was Gene a big Beatles fan?

That was a lot of fun. I had known Gene since *Beatlemania* rehearsals at SIR in NYC in 1976. KISS were in the next studio rehearsing for a tour. Gene and Paul came in and being the big Beatle fans they were, put us through our paces. Four hours singing for them. We were in LA ending the show's run at the Shubert in Century City before moving to the Blackstone Theater in Chicago.

You also went on to write quite a bit for Kiss. Would you tell us what that was like for you?

After years of knowing each other but not seeing each other much, one 4th of July at a rooftop barbecue at Peppy Castro's house, I ran into Paul Stanley. We had a great time, basically talking nonstop for the time we were there. He gave me his phone number and said call him. The next morning when I woke up found and the number, I froze. I never called him. And the next year at the same event, he asks me "Why didn't you call?" I said, "Because I said to myself I can't call Paul Stanley!" He punched me in the arm and said, "Don't do that again!" We laughed and got on famously for years. He, Gene and I used to hang out a lot. Together and individually. I wrote stuff for *Creatures of the Night* and more that was never used. But when *Animalize* came around, I had 3 co-writes.

So, is Paul still with us? Where do you cast your vote?
    My vote's he's with us in spades!

Mickey Leigh

Mickey Leigh is a musician, and brother of Joey Ramone.

Please tell us about yourself, and what you've been up to, will you please?
    My name is Mickey Leigh. Born, raised and still living in Forest Hills, Queens. I started playing the guitar in 1965 when I was 10. Formed a band (Purple Majesty) and started writing songs at 11. Recorded two songs with them when we were 12, which were recently released by Norton Records. I'm still playing, have a band called Mickey Leigh's Mutated Music and had 6 singles released by Steven Van Zandt on his label, Wicked Cool Records, in 2020 & 21, and an album called *Variants Of Vibe* released in February of 2022. I also wrote a book about growing up with my brother, called *I Slept With Joey Ramone* published by Simon & Schuster.

When did you first become aware of the Beatles, and how long did it take before they had you hooked?
    My brother and I were into music, mainly rock 'n' roll, since the days we were in our single digits, we were already listening to the WMCA Good Guys, Murray the K, and Cousin Brucie on our little 8 transistor radios, constantly even prior to the British Invasion. Whatever they played, we loved it. From the Four Seasons to Stevie Wonder to the Beach Boys. But, when we heard about this band from England that was doing something unheard of to that point, we had to find out what it was all about. For a week or so, we only saw pictures of them. Finally we heard them on the radio. How long did it take before they had us hooked? ....maybe 10 seconds.

Did any of the Beatles become your favorite, and why did that Beatle appeal to you?

I really didn't have a "favorite" Beatle. I think girls were more inclined to have a favorite Beatle, the one they'd swoon to more than the others. I didn't swoon over them. I just thought they were the coolest bunch of guys I'd ever seen, heard or wanted to be like.

As a musician, how did the Beatles influence you as a songwriter and player?

I wouldn't use the word "did". I'd say "do". ...still. Perpetually. They influenced me in ways far beyond anyone else had to that point. Their spirit and personalities were what really changed me. Everything about them was fun. I loved the songs, the look, and the sound, but I think I was just as equally affected by their humor and the way they answered questions in interviews. When you ask me "how did the Beatles influence you as a songwriter and player?", my reply is "I really don't know. You'd probably have to ask them how they did that." ...see what I mean?

Can you tell us about when you first heard of the rumors that Paul McCartney was said to have been replaced by a double named Billy Shears?

I heard DJ Scott Muni on WNEW FM breaking the story on his show. I didn't buy it. I honestly never took it seriously for a second. I was only 15 in 1969 but I'd already been working as a messenger in Midtown and traveling down to the West Village with my friends. I'd encountered kinda scam from hippies trying to sell us the powers of salvation that lay inside their seashells that fell from outer space, and subjected to every con and scam artist in the city. When I heard them trying to push that story, I smelled a seashell from space. But, was still semi-intrigued.

Did you ever play your vinyl records backwards looking for 'clues'?

ABSOLUTELY. Not looking for "proof," but just to hear those things. It was fun!

The Beatles are said to have used album cover art to tell us what had happened to Paul. Which ones stand out to you?

Of course, *Abbey Road* on which he's walking barefoot. And...

Using your musician's ear, which audio 'clues' in the songs resonate with you?

Not that they were very musical, but we were really only able to *clearly* hear the "I buried Paul" line out of all the ones we attempted to hear. I suppose it also depended on how skilled the person was at spinning vinyl backwards.

Some say the Beatles stopped touring because Paul was replaced. As a veteran musician, why do you suspect that the Beatles stopped touring?

I never heard they stopped touring because Paul was being replaced, but that their record label dropped him for writing too many hit songs.

So, is Paul still with us? Where do you cast your vote?

I conclude that not only is Paul still with us, but that the fascination created by the rumor of his death combined with a faction of people relentlessly dedicating their lives to proving it paved the way for, what today is called, Qanon?

Mike Williams

Mike Williams is known popularly on line as the Sage of Quay. His writings and podcasts cover a variety of controversial topics. He has explored the "Paul is Dead" phenomenon in great detail.

Please tell us all about yourself?

I have been researching various conspiracy topics for over 12 years. In 2011 I decided to create my blog, Sage of Quay Radio (https://sageofquayblog.blogspot.com/) as a vehicle to present alternative research and information to the public. Then in 2014, I began podcasting and interviewing many researchers on a wide array of topics to help disseminate alternative viewpoints to a wider audience. In 2016 I began my research into the McCartney (Paul is Dead) and Beatle conspiracy after reading the book *The Memoirs of Billy Shears*. Initially, I planned on two to three interviews to discuss the topic but the more I researched the deeper the rabbit hole became and I realized the conspiracy was (and still is) a major psychological operation that was created by the deep state to social engineer the world. Before my alternative research endeavors, I worked in the corporate world for over 30 years. After my corporate career, I was in private practice for 12 years as a master hypnotherapist which I recently retired from. I am also a musician and songwriter (http://laboroflovemusic.com/). Anyone interested in my work can find the links to all my platforms on my hub website: http://sageofquay.com/

When did you first discover the Beatles?

I was fully aware of the Beatles by the time I was 9 years old in 1968. I remember asking my parents to take me to the local movie theater to see *Yellow Submarine*. My father took me and my brother to see the movie. I was a huge Beatle fan.

Did you have a favorite Beatle? If so, why?

Growing up my favorite Beatles were Paul and John because they were the primary songwriters of the music I grew up with and loved.

How did you first hear about the legend that Paul was dead?

I remember discussing the topic with my friends back in 1976 when I was in high school (we were all Beatle fans). We would learn about the album clues and then look for them. We would also listen for the audio clues embedded in the songs. I don't recall any of us actually believing Paul was dead. At the time, I thought of the clues as an entertaining game or puzzle the Beatles created for their fans. Later on, I thought of the clues as a clever marketing ploy to sell more records (which actually did happen). It wasn't until 2016, after reading *The Memoirs of Billy Shears* (by Thomas E. Uharriet), that I realized the topic (i.e., the replacement of McCartney and the Beatles as an entity) was part of an overall internationalist agenda to breakdown traditional values and the prevailing religious institutions (predominantly Christianity) in order to transition the world to a one world governance.

What clues first drew your interest to this?

Back in the late 1970s, the album covers clues were fun to look for, in particular from the *Abbey Road, Sgt. Pepper* and *Magical Mystery Tour* albums as well as the audio clues contained within the songs (e.g., *Revolution 9*'s "turn me on dead man", *Strawberry Fields'* "I buried Paul", etc.) Then after reading *The Memoirs of Billy Shears* back in 2016 (the first edition was published September 9, 2009), and taking in the extraordinary level of detailed information contained in the book, I thought this could only have come from a person or persons who have an intimate knowledge of the Beatles and the inner workings of the band. I believe that person to be Billy Shears (aka Shepherd/Campbell) who is the person playing the role of Paul McCartney (as the primary replacement) since September of 1966 (the book, which is written in first person, tells us that biological Paul died September 11, 1966). *Memoirs* is classified as historical fiction but per the book, this was done in order to navigate around legal constraints as a result of non-disclosure and secrecy agreements to which Billy is bound (as well as the author/encoder Thomas Uharriet). However, the book reveals an enormous amount of truth if the reader is intrepid enough to study and decode the book's content. As an example, *Memoirs* contains three layers of narrative which when brought together lead the reader closer to the truth as well as inviting the reader to use the book as a stepping stone to pursue research outside the book to both validate the content and uncover the hidden (i.e., real) story of the Beatles. I explain to my subscribers that *Memoirs* is like solving a complex puzzle. It takes time and patience (the book is 666 pages). After six years of studying the book's content and researching the conspiracy as a whole, I along with my fellow researchers feel we have made significant progress in understanding the conspiracy at a level that goes far beyond Paul McCartney being replaced. In fact, I have said that the McCartney and Beatles conspiracy is so deep that the swapping out of Paul McCartney has become a subplot.

Please give us the case for Paul McCartney dying and being replaced in the Beatles.

The best case for Paul being replaced by Billy is to read the *Memoirs of Billy Shears* (the entire story is laid out and explained in detail) as well as watching my content at https://jamespaulmccartney. com/ where I break down the many facets of the conspiracy. However, in short, a completely different person emerges with the release of *Sgt. Pepper* in 1967. The differences are not just the physical attributes but also in personality. The physical differences include Billy being taller than Paul by a few inches and having a longer, narrower face ("Man, you been a naughty boy you let your face grow long" – *I Am the Walrus*). They also have different ears. The differences in facial characteristics can be detected when images of "McCartney" are examined side-by-side over a timeline. For example, compare images of McCartney from the 1962 through 1966 period with images of Billy during his Wings period. They are not the same person. Since most people have never performed a side-by-side comparison they just assume Billy is Paul because that is who they are told he is (and people see what they expect to see). It should also be pointed out that not all of the images from the 1962 through 1966 period are of biological Paul since doubles, look-alikes and image doctoring are in the mix. So, it takes a keen eye and discernment to understand who you are looking at. Per *Memoirs*, one way to do the comparisons is to refer to the early album covers which the book tells are of the real Paul McCartney.

Another comparison is to look at the differences in their stance and movements when Paul and Billy play the bass. Watch performance videos of Paul and compare his movements and stance with Billy's when he's performing (e.g., the rooftop scene from the *Get Back* sessions). How they stand and move when playing is quite different. When Paul played his bass, he would occasionally glance down at his fret hand whereas Billy, because he is naturally right-handed, looks more frequently at the fretboard to see where he is on the neck of the guitar. Another anomaly is McCartney's piano skills. Prior to 1967, Paul McCartney was not known for his piano playing. Yet starting in 1967 we have a version of McCartney who is a very accomplished piano player (e.g., *Martha My Dear*, *Lady Madonna*, etc.) These are just some quick examples of differences in physical attributes and mannerisms. However, their personalities are also very different. Paul often displayed a reserved personality while Billy is more outspoken and projects an outgoing, self-assured, and confident persona (some say there is an arrogance about him). To better see the differences in personality, study interviews of Paul from the early Beatle period and then view interviews of Billy starting in 1967 through the current day. If you watch with an open mind, it should become obvious, that they are two different people.

How would you explain the unlikelihood of finding someone that looks so much like Paul the world was fooled, played guitar left-handed, sang like Paul, and was such a great songwriter?

Billy was transformed to look like Paul via plastic and cosmetic surgery which included fillers (to fill out the face), reproducing scars, dying his body hair, wearing wigs, and the use of latex. Billy is Scottish and his natural hair color is reddish-blonde. In *Memoirs*, he tells us that if we want to know what he looked like before the transformation, we should look to his son, James, who resembles him. To bridge the gap as Billy was transitioning to "Paul", "McCartney" doubles and look-alikes (actors) were used for public consumption. From the very beginning, all of the Beatles deployed a number of doubles and look-alikes throughout the entire timeline spanning both their Beatle and solo careers. *Memoirs* tells us Billy still uses a double. I have an interview on my channel where Mike Campbell and Bentmont Tench from The Heartbreakers (Tom Petty's band) talk about Ringo's double who they claim looks exactly like him. That video can be found here: https://youtu.be/ boNRJnbCsoA. Since Billy was placed within the context of the Beatles and in the role of Paul McCartney, the public sees him as Paul McCartney. Otherwise, who else could he be?

Billy made his official debut as a Beatle with the release of *Sgt Pepper* back in June of 1967. In order to disguise the difference in physical appearances between Paul and Billy, Tavistock (i.e., the deep state/controllers) dramatically changed the look of the band as they emerged with longer hair, beards, and mustaches as well as donning psychedelic attire. The new Beatles (with Billy at the helm) were a sharp contrast to the look of the pre-1967 Beatles. Altering the appearance of the entire band helped to take the focus off of Billy. Since all of the Beatles looked very different, it wasn't just "Paul" who changed. By deploying and photographing multiple doubles and look-alikes over the timeline, a composite image of Paul McCartney was established in the minds of the public who were conditioned to accept the current version (look) of McCartney as Paul McCartney. Since very few people took the time (or cared) to go back and scrutinize and question the obvious discrepancies, the task of covering up became easier with time as Billy established himself in the role.

As I mentioned earlier, Billy is naturally right-handed and this was confirmed to me by a source within the music business who witnessed him playing right-handed in the studio back in the 1980s. Although switching from playing right-handed to left-handed is not an easy task, it is certainly not impossible. With determination and motivation, it can be done and Billy was highly motivated since he had to play left-handed to be "Paul McCartney". There are Beatle tribute bands where the musician playing the Paul character switched from their natural right-handed playing to lefty in order to bring a more authentic presentation to the audience. It should also be noted (per *Memoirs*) that when Billy records he does so by playing right-handed. His left-handed persona is reserved for public events such as concerts, shows, etc. I remember years ago, reading an article by a music critic who questioned why McCartney's bass playing during concerts was not as intricate as his recordings. The reason is that Billy needed to simplify some of the bass work in order to pull off the bass part when he plays left-handed.

Back in 1968, Dr. Henry Truby who was a professor at the University of Miami and an expert in linguistics and voiceprint (sonogram) analysis decided to compare *Yesterday* with *Penny Lane* as well as comparing *Yesterday* with *Hey Jude*. Per *Memoirs*, Dr. Truby was looking to prove that Paul McCartney was always Paul McCartney. However, after doing the analysis he found the person singing *Yesterday* is not the same vocalist on *Penny Lane* or *Hey Jude (Yesterday* was sung by Paul and both *Penny Lane* and *Hey Jude* are Billy songs). In the November 7, 1969 edition of *Life* magazine, there is an article titled "The Magical McCartney Mystery" where the Paul is Dead conspiracy is discussed (with an obvious bias toward debunking the premise). In that article, at the bottom of pages 104 and 105, they present a blurb about Dr. Truby's findings. The caption reads: "Dr. Henry Truby of the University of Miami found Sonograms of Paul singing *Hey Jude* of last year (1968) suspiciously different from the phrase "all my troubles" from *Yesterday*, done earlier. Could there have been more than one "McCartney"?" Unfortunately, *Life* magazine does not expand on Dr. Truby's credentials as an expert in the field of linguistics and voiceprint analysis or dig deeper into his findings. Voiceprints are considered unique to each person just like fingerprints and are used by law enforcement to help identify people suspected of a crime. But even without the voiceprints, a discerning ear can hear the difference in Paul's voice when compared to Billy's singing. Paul sang from the throat whereas Billy sings properly from the diaphragm. Unlike Paul, Billy is a formally trained singer, songwriter. and multi-instrumentalist who can read and write music (Paul coulc not). His primary instruments are wind and the piano. And as we know he's also skilled at playing the guitar, bass, and drums (and Billy drums right-handed). On the cover of *Sgt. Pepper*, you will see each Beatle holding a wind instrument which represents the various wind instruments Billy plays. Billy also tells us in *Memoirs* that before his Beatle days he was a studio musician as well as a vocal impersonator. He would be hired to do studio recordings where he was asked to sing and sound like another (more famous) singer. So, voice mimicry is a skill he possesses. Just like the creation of a composite Paul McCartney from a visual perspective, the same phenomenon is in play with his voice. Over time it all becomes intertwined and a blur. And, we must keep in mind that it is Billy's voice we have been listening to for over 56 years and not Paul who was in the official Beatle timeline for only four years from 1962 through 1966.

Back in April of 2020, I released a 4.5-hour presentation titled "Did the Beatles Write All Their Own Music" (https://youtu.be/ ccEhmQ0M4FY) where I present evidence that the Beatles did not write all their own music and they did not play on all of the recorded tracks. The music was written by ghostwriters (led in all likelihood by Theodor Adorno and George Martin) and the instrumental tracks were recorded by studio musicians. The Beatles' role was to sing the songs (just like the Monkees). This is especially true during the biological Paul period which ran from 1962 through 1966. Starting in 1967 with *Sgt. Pepper* (and Billy running the band), John Lennon, and George Harrison contributed more to the songwriting efforts and played on some of the recorded tracks but ghostwriters and studio musicians were still being used to create Beatle albums and singles. I came to this conclusion after analyzing the official narrative behind the making of *Rubber Soul* where we are told the Beatles came in with no backlog of music and then proceeded to write, rehearse, arrange and record 16 songs in 30 days between October 11, 1965 and November 11, 1965. A daunting task to say the least. The 16 songs were comprised of 14 songs for the album and two additional songs for a double A-side single. The goal was to have *Rubber Soul* in stores by December 3, 1965, for the Christmas season. The release of an album cannot effectively begin until the final lacquer is completed which took place on November 17, 1965. This left approximately 2.5 weeks to pull together the record labels, artwork, printing, album sleeves, and distribution in order to package the album and make the December 3rd date. Even if EMI (the Beatles label) had pulled out all the stops to expedite the release of *Rubber Soul* (at the expense of other EMI artists with Christmas album releases) the cycle time to get the album out would have taken a minimum of 6 weeks with 8-weeks being the norm. Yet, *Rubber Soul* was out the door and in stores in 2.5 weeks.

There are many more problems with the *Rubber Soul* narrative which I cover in my big presentation but the entire scenario of coming in with no backlog of songs and then recording 16 in 30 days coupled with highly questionable time frames to produce and distribute the record lead me to conclude there was a template used by George Martin for all of the Beatles' records, especially with the first seven albums (the biological Paul period), starting with *Please Please Me* (their debut album released March 22, 1963) through *Revolver* (released on August 5, 1966). The Beatles' 30 days in the studio to record *Rubber Soul* meant they had 30 days to record the vocals. Thus, by the time the Beatles arrived in the studio on October 11th all of the songs were already written and recorded and the only thing left to do was to add the vocal tracks. Since the songs were already written and recorded beforehand, the names of the songs, the run times, sequencing, record labels, artwork, and manufacturing of the record sleeves were in the bag waiting for the Beatles to complete the vocals. Once the vocals were done George Martin did the final mix and then sent the recordings off to be mastered, pressed to vinyl, and packaged. It was the only way *Rubber Soul* could have been in stores 2.5 weeks after the final lacquer was cut on November 17, 1965.

It is also well worth the time to watch my presentation on the 1960 through 1963 period to understand how the Beatles were handled and managed through the startup stages of their timeline in order to place them where they needed to be when Tavistock decided to throw the switch on the psychological operation known to the world as *Beatlemania*. That video can be found here: https://youtu. be/IBV_j-pZgag

The answer to the question of how they were able to replace a great songwriter like Paul is easy. Paul McCartney and John Lennon were not prolific and great songwriters. It's a myth. It's a fictional story that millions of fans embrace without inspecting and questioning the official narrative. It's a Cinderella story that most people accept at face value. John Lennon, Paul McCartney, George Harrison, and Ringo Starr were performers who brought Tavistock's *Beatlemania* social engineering initiative to the world stage. They were not great songwriters and they were not great musicians. Thus, replacing Paul with Billy who was (and is) an experienced and skilled composer was not a complicated task.

How have people responded to you believing that the real Paul McCartney died in 1966?

Of course, my research does not sit well with Beatle fans. However, there are also many critical thinkers who understand all the world is a stage and that the music and entertainment industry is completely controlled from top to bottom with music being a major tool in the toolbox of the controllers which is used to shape and condition the minds of the masses. A number of years ago on a podcast I was hosting I said to my guest "anything worth knowing is a lie" and that includes the Beatles.

Do you entertain the possibility that you might be wrong about this?

I am 100% convinced the person playing Paul McCartney today and since 1966 is not the original Paul McCartney. Biological Paul is gone and for 56 years we have been watching and listening to the one and only Billy Shears!

So cast your vote officially - is Paul still with us?

No, biological James Paul McCartney is no longer with us.

Joseph Brutsman

Joseph Brutsman is an actor whose many screen credits include a recurring role on the television series *Scarecrow and Mrs. King*. He has worked extensively as a producer, most recently for the TV documentary series *Lara Logan Has no Agenda*. He recently published the book *Marlon & Greg: My Life and Filmmaking Adventures with Hollywood's Polar Opposites,* which recounts his work with acting legends Marlon Brando and Gregory Peck.

Please tell us about yourself and your work.

In my recent book, *Marlon & Greg*, I tell of my many years writing and producing with and for Marlon Brando and Gregory Peck. I knew them well in their final years, and much of my book is about the highs, lows and flat-out bizarre nature of extreme fame; the kind of epic fame that can transcend categorization. Were Peck and Brando mere "actors"? Don't tell that to filmgoers who feel their lives have been enriched, enhanced or even transformed by those men. Were the Beatles just a band? You're reading this book, so I think you know the answer to that. In that aforementioned book of mine, the Beatles receive a special mention as I attempt to describe the crazy atom-smash of historic timing, pop culture randomness and the incalculable set of odds that shape the arrival and survival of the extremely famous. With perhaps a slight excess of candor, I confess to being what many of we fully lapsed Catholics are: a present day agnostic. But do I believe in miracles? Well, that's where I bring the Beatles into my conversation.

Here's how I put it: to me personally, I have no better definition of a "Miracle" than the Beatles. These four guys, coming together, when they did, how they did, mixing their talents the way they did, for that generation at that time, leaving behind so much joy, emotion and love; magical music that will surely last forever - Or, at least, until some unforeseen generation says, "Who cares about those guys?" That ending sounds impossible to some; likely to others. And so what? That's the march of time at work; we can't fight it, stop it, or at times, remotely understand it. But still, while they were here, while their music still lasts, the Beatles - those four individuals - who they were and what they did; they make me believe in "miracles" far beyond any Scripture in any existing religion. Yes, I know John, Paul, George and Ringo were mere mortals, but "The Beatles" - C'mon, nothing short of "4-planet-aligning" miraculous. And frankly, they were bathed in the kind of fame that would easily feed the "Paul is Dead" story and rumor.

One morning in the 1990's, my wife Avra and I heard something on the radio about Marlon Brando having passed away last night. This was news to us. Avra was Marlon's assistant. I often wrote screenplays with Marlon, and we had just seen him mere hours ago, last night. When he didn't answer his phone, we quickly went up to his house. He was a sound sleeper, but with this "news", we took it upon ourselves to storm the castle and make sure we could find him safely sleeping and breathing in his bed. We did. When Avra woke him up and told him what we had heard, he loudly laughed. He then immediately became quite serious, telling us both, "Don't you dare tell anyone that it's not true!" First his laugh and then that command: both pure Marlon. When we asked if he knew how such fiction became "news", he muttered, "'No idea. 'Happens every few years." And with that, he told us to leave as he calmly went back to sleep. With a smile. So, why would those bizarre things happen to legends like Brando and McCartney and not mere mortals such as ourselves? I think the answer is somewhere in the area of how much the public loves these artists. We're afraid of losing them. Perhaps those odd hoaxes are almost trial runs for that very sad day when they really will leave us. I recall thinking that on the day that Marlon died. I didn't want to believe it was true.

As for Paul, it seems that he will somehow live forever. Unless, of course, he's already long gone.

How did you first become aware of the Beatles, and how long before you were hooked on them?

I was a toddler when the Beatles first hit the U.S. My father made his living playing piano bar seven nights a week in the Midwest; of course he didn't "get" the Beatles - He barely "got" Elvis, playing to an audience that loved Bing. Sinatra, country western and even polka. In short: the Beatles weren't on the household hi-fi when I was very young, in the early 60's. But as an avid animation freak, I loved the Beatles animated series, mostly about girls chasing the guys and goofy Ringo getting into ridiculous situations. I was six by the time *Sgt. Pepper* came out, and clearly, their new wild look and sound confused and infuriated my lounge musician father even more. By then, I had learned about and loved the "Mop-Top" Beatles, but their "new" songs and costumes said only one thing to my parents and to their generation: "DRUGS!" Yes, it felt as though those innocent mop-tops in the matching suits had now found drugs; the trippy cover of *Sgt. Pepper* said it all. Almost on cue, NBC unleashed their rip-off, "The Monkees" onto the airwaves, and I'll never forget the words of my older sister; as she watched my younger sister and me grapple with these "new" scary "druggie" Beatles, she informed us, "They're done! Now, if you're a cool kid, you like the Monkees instead!" So said my sister Pam at the wise old age of eight.

As a wannabe artist, I loved the *Sgt. Pepper* cover, especially seeing the old mop-tops standing next to the "new" *Pepper*

Beatles. Contrary to what my elder sister told me, even at the age of six, I did sense that the Beatles probably had more texture, nuance and weight than the Monkees, even as the top 40 radio music stations of the day often played far more Monkees than Beatles - Ah, the fickle and bizarre nature of pop culture. Yes, I know what you are saying: "How the hell are the Monkees even in this conversation?" Good point. Again, I was six; even Fred Flintstone was still in my world at that time. Of course, that WAS the amazing, across-the-board fame of the Beatles - here they were: my parents (not fans) were still talking about when they were on *Ed Sullivan*, they had already been a part of my young Saturday morning cartoon watching, and here they were with this *Sgt. Pepper* evolution, already reinventing themselves, just as I was still trying learn who they really were. By the time I was ten, in 1970, I was fully hooked, and the day I heard they were breaking up; that was a sad day I could not believe. Back then, in a non-Internet era, I really didn't keep up with any entertainment news or gossip about whether they were fighting, whether or not they were getting along, or whether or not they had planned on staying together forever. Years back, I of course DID hear the things about Paul possibly being dead, but once those rumors were put to rest, I didn't give them much thought. Today, I believe rumors like that have an endless life thanks to the Internet. Back then, yes, I'm sure there were young adults that kept believing, finding new "clues" and even creating whatever they needed to keep the "Paul is Dead" story alive. As a young kid, once I heard he was alive, I went with that, not feeling any "death" sorrow until I heard the band was breaking up. Many years later, I arrived at Juilliard and got an apartment not all that far from where John Lennon lived off Central Park West. One day, the streets near my apartment were blocked; crowds gathered. Lennon had been shot. Of course, everyone SO hoped that the news that day - like all that old Paul stuff - was just a hoax.

Did any of the Beatles stand out to you as a favorite? Why did that person resonate with you?

I don't believe I ever thought once of having a "favorite" Beatle; that's what seemed so amazing about the four of them together - They were all so different, they somehow balanced each other out; what can I say? Together, they were the perfect quartet. But leave it to my friends, Wilson and Jeffries, to ask the tough questions. When they wanted to know if I could personally put one of the lads in some sort of "First Place" position, I frankly shocked myself as I squinted into the distance and muttered, "Of course, - George." It's the kind of answer that then has you asking yourself, "Why?" I've read that when such polls are conducted today, Paul usually wins by a mile. Cut his poll number in half - With that number, you then get a close tie between John and George, and then Ringo usually trails close behind. I'm certain there's a test or two out there, especially online - Some sort of, "What does your favorite Beatle tell you about YOU?" Okay, regarding my Harrison selection, I'll give it a few guesses. I do love that he was the "Quiet" Beatle. When I first heard the cool guitar leads in the early songs, even at a young age, I recall being shocked to learn that was George; after all, it did seem that the "Other Guitar Player" was the "leader" of the band. He was. But George was lead guitar. Jumping ahead here - How great was it for George to foster skilled filmmakers with his "Handmade Films" company? Every project was a work of passion and art, even the films that failed miserably, all getting to the screen because of George Harrison.

But let's first go back to the Beatles and that period where John and Paul were then learning that authorship on an album was becoming a three-way divide. We know the titles and we know that soft voice that was finally heard after too many years of doing only harmony work. Of course, he's also the one that opened up the world to the others; Harrison's investigations of different cultures, inspirations and even continents - It's never been in dispute: it was George who led the others to those new and fascinating places. Who would have thought that it was "The Quiet One" who was The World Citizen of the pack? Perhaps it was that unpredictability of Harrison that seemed so intriguing. After the Beatles, his work and his projects were always interesting, whether George was doing charity work, collaborating with old friends or producing movies. A truly amazing man.

You have a great book from Bear Manor, called Marlon & Greg. *How did Marlon Brando influence the Beatles' name?*

I've been told that a theory about Marlon and the "Beatle" name surfaced around the time of the release of the '95 Anthology project. John Lennon and the best friend of his youth, Stu Sutcliffe, were huge Brando fans. Given that, not surprisingly, they especially loved Marlon's ode to rebellion, *The Wild One*. Sutcliffe was Lennon's influential pal from Art College. Stu's girlfriend, Astrid, reportedly came up with the Beatles' famous hairstyles. Any good Lennon historian knows how shaken John was when Stu tragically died of a brain hemorrhage at the youthful age of 21. *The Wild One* came out in '53. In a pivotal scene from the film, Lee Marvin and his biker gang roll into the small town that has been occupied by Brando and his gang, "The Black Rebels Motorcycle Club". As it must be with such restless young characters, push does indeed come to shove, as Marvin's character ruthlessly taunts Brando's character, Johnny Strabler. Johnny throws him to the ground! Marvin then says, "We missed ya, Johnny! The beetles missed ya! All the beetles missed ya!" Some say this quote was an influence on the name of the group. Fuel to that fire is added when one recalls the Brando *Wild One* photo pictured amongst the legendary group on the crowded *Sgt. Pepper* album cover. Interestingly, in my book, I tell a bit about how Marlon didn't quite "Get" the Beatles; perhaps it was a generational thing. But he also didn't love the music of Elvis Presley either. Jazz and Latin music - Those were his true loves. When he did say that he liked *Rocky Raccoon*, I asked Avra about it. She suspected his mention probably came purely from the fact that Marlon once had a pet raccoon, and perhaps that was that.

You are a graduate of Juilliard, and are well-versed concerning Hollywood. What do you think about the Beatles and the films that they made?

Let's face it, the Beatles were too big NOT to make movies - whether they liked it or not. Like the film career of Elvis, the output is, understandably, a mixed bag. But unlike Presley, it seemed as though the Beatles had no hardcore "pursuit" of movie stardom, making their few films all the more interesting, and making *A Hard Day's Night* into something of a miracle. Richard Lester deserves a lot of the credit for this magical mix of comedy, music and (let's call it what it fully was at the time) flat-out exploitation of a worldwide phenomena. To me, it's one of those rare films that gets better and better as time goes on; thank God we have it. There they are - So young, funny and talented - All in glorious black and white. For me, their next-best: the recent *The Beatles: Get Back.*

When did you first become aware that Paul McCartney was said to be replaced in the Beatles, and was singing with the angels?

Thinking back, it's amazing to think that even in my small-town Minnesota grade school, kids talked about the "Dead Paul" rumors and all the "facts" behind that. This, in an age long before the Internet. Frankly, that speaks to the epic power and fame of the Beatles, as well as to (perhaps) the "stoner" set that was the generation directly ahead of me. I recall kids telling me all about the many "clues". I'd ask, "Where did you hear this?" I'd often hear answers such as, "From my older brother - him and his friends were hanging out the other night, talking all about it." Right or wrong, even at the age of ten, when I heard about older kids, teens, "hanging out" and kicking around strange theories about rock stars, well, I kinda assumed there was something in the air at that "meeting".

What did you make of the "clues" that Paul was departed on the album covers?

After a while, one would lose track about which clue was what - The bare feet, the cigarette in which hand, the definition of "Walrus", who is wearing white and who is wearing black, the VW license plate - Egad! Yes, I suppose I should keep an open mind regarding all this, but more to the point, as you might sense, I'm more intrigued with how and why such fables get created, promoted, and perhaps most mysteriously - believed.

There were also "clues" in the songs, as well. Did you ever play any of your vinyl records backwards?

I feel I might ruin my albums if I played them backwards, so, no, I've never done that. I guess in recording or DJ work, they call it, what? "Back-masking"? Yeah? All that nutty backward-recording and playback. BUT - frankly, think about how great something like that was back in the days of the Beatles. Seriously. Commercial and pop music were trying different things; not just some small underground act. No, the Beatles themselves were utilizing new and radical techniques, painting fully abstract works of audio art in a recording studio. It really was a bold new era. Nobody thought they were getting hidden, secret messages out of *Twist and Shout, A Hard Day's Night* or even *Yesterday*.

What do you make of the many records released, and all of the solo shows by Paul?

This would be quite a feat for the imposter, wouldn't it? After George Harrison died, a friend of mine said, "Now only the boring Beatles are alive." Somehow, I found that statement to be both vulgar and understandable at the exact same time. Paul and Ringo were always the "relatable" ones - The Cute One and The Funny One. Simplistic labels to be sure, but strange how those notions stuck to those men for so long. Lennon and Harrison were both phantoms of a sort; George with his mysterious presence - John with his commanding talent and imposing legend; of course, his tragic death only added to that image. What point am I getting to? I believe it is this: Paul McCartney is a singular and special talent; no imposter could have come along and accomplished what he's done - during the Beatles or after. That is obvious. What seems less obvious to some: McCartney has so clearly been given a bit of a bad rap post-Beatles - Hell, it's why he wrote pieces like *Silly Love Songs* - That was his answer to critics who thought he wasn't as "deep" as John, he was the "Cute" one - Later, he was the one who was far too wealthy. Even many Beatle fans still fall into the same notions: John was the genius, George was the dark, quiet genius, Ringo was the showman, the entertainer; Starr's on his own level; he's something of his own invention. But PAUL? Oh, so commercial, too successful, a Knighthood, owning castles, so many pop bubblegum songs, etc. Thankfully, today, most of the world sees him as the icon that he clearly is — He needs nobody to say this, but Paul McCartney is a brilliant composer, an amazing lyricist, a legendary singer, the world's most famous bassist, an incredible guitarist, an accomplished pianist, a needed optimist, a loving husband, a devoted father, and one of the greatest live performers of our time. He's brought joy to billions of people for so many decades. Frankly, anyone who wants to waste time hating on this guy needs to step back and, perhaps, have a good, hard look at their own life.

So, is Paul still with us? Where do you cast your vote?

Maybe I should pull a crazy move now and say, "As much as I've been sounding like I find all this 'Paul is Dead' stuff to be hogwash, - No, I do believe otherwise; with this much evidence, there could be truth to it." But no, not for me. He lives. Paul is not dead.

Bob Cowsill

Bob Cowsill played guitar and organ for the popular 1960s family band The Cowsills.

Please tell us about yourself, and what you have been up to.

I'm Bob Cowsill of The Cowsills family singing group. We just
released our album *Rhythm of the World* on Omnivore Recordings
on 9.30.22. We launched "The Cowsills Podcast" during the
pandemic shutdown and have 62 episodes up on demand with a new
guest and new episode every Wednesday. We tour every summer
with The Happy Together Tour and are part of the annual Christmas
show in Branson, Missouri at the Andy Williams Moon River
Theater Nov 1 - Dec 9th plus perform on The Flower Power cruise
and in venues across America.

*When did you first become aware of the Beatles, and how long did it
take for you to become a fan?*

I became aware at the age of 13 or 14 when me and my brother
Billy watched them play *You Can't Do That* on *The Jack Paar* show
late one night. We had our own band with our younger brothers and
at the time we were into Ricky Nelson, The Everly Brothers and
very big on the folk music scene. The Beatles changed everything
and at our age we were perfect human "sponges" for all of it. We
learned what to wear, what gear to buy (Ludwig, Gretsch, Hofner
became household words in our house), they showed us what songs
to learn and if you played those songs good enough you got work.
They taught us about songwriting that we could also be songwriters
too....that anyone can write a song. We listened to their records
trying to figure it all out....how they were doing what they were
doing. Listening to their records was our only recourse until the
three appearances on *The Ed Sullivan Show* ... School was in!!! We
got 3 consecutive Sundays, maybe about 12 songs and we were off
and running.

*Did you have a favorite Beatle, and why did they stand out to
you?*

McCartney was my favorite. Loved his voice the most and his
vocal flexibility.

The Cowsills and The Beatles did nifty covers of the Marvelettes' Please Mr. Postman. - *Which is your favorite version?*

The Beatles version of anything would be my favorite. We don't compare to the Beatles and no one else has to either. They were number one...uncontested. The rest of us could fight each other for number two but nobody was going to unseat the Beatles during our time.

You also did a rocking Tell Me Why. *What are your thoughts on that song?*

Tell Me Why is one of the most difficult Beatle songs to perform and sing...you have to be in really good shape for that one... and really nobody does. We could handle it but we were just playing in a pub singing songs like that; we did a ton of Beatle songs and we were quite good at sounding like the Beatles even at a young age.

When did you first become aware of the rumors that Paul McCartney was replaced by Billy Shears?

Probably sometime in '69.

Did the Cowsills ever have any conversations about Paul's supposed demise?

Oh we were all over that whole thing...playing Number 9 backwards the "I buried Paul" at the end of the fadeout in *Strawberry Fields Forever*; the Abbey Road procession, we loved the whole thing. One day my son, Jason, was looking into the whole thing and he got caught up in the historic clues everyone knew about...now that's something.

Which 'clues' stand out to you from the album covers?

Well there's sort of a "grave" on *Sgt. Pepper* and of course the *Abbey Road* cover with the whole cigarette in the right hand, out of step with the other three, etc. Crazy.

Did you ever play your vinyl records backwards? Which audio clues stand out in your thoughts?

Totally blown away by the "I buried Paul" and "the Walrus was Paul" given in a clue setting. We have an instrumental part on an old song from an old album where we turned the guitar instrumental backwards and used it that way....in a song called *Contact Mae* from our *On My Side* album.

So, is Paul still with us? Where do you cast your vote?

Oh he's with us alright. He's part of a small group of stars who honestly love to perform. He never wanted to stop performing and he never did.

Bruce Spizer

Bruce Spizer is the author of many books on the Beatles, and is considered the definitive expert on the phenomenon of *Beatlemania*.

Will you please tell us about yourself (bio), your work, and what new projects are coming up? Feel free to plug your work here!!!

Bruce Spizer is a Beatles author/historian who has written and published 14 books on the Beatles. The original series of books dealt with the Beatles' records on various record labels, included books covering Vee-Jay, Capitol, Apple and Swan. Another book covered the British releases on Parlophone. Bruce also wrote the definitive book on *Beatlemania* in America, *The Beatles Are Coming! The Birth of Beatlemania in America*. Beginning in 2017, he wrote and published the book *The Beatles and Sgt. Pepper: A Fans' Perspective*. It would become the first in a series of books on the Beatles albums. Later titles include *The Beatles White Album and the Launch of Apple*, *The Beatles Get Back to Abbey Road*, *The Beatles Finally Let It Be*, *The Beatles Magical Mystery Tour and Yellow Submarine* and *The Beatles Rubber Soul to Revolver*. Bruce is a frequent guest at Beatles conventions through the United States and had made presentations on the Beatles at the Rock and Roll Hall of Fame and

Museum, the Grammy Museum, the American Film Institute, the Lincoln Center and other venues. Bruce does consulting work for Universal Music Group, Capitol Records and Apple Corps Ltd. He maintains the website www.beatle.net

When did you first see the Beatles, and when were you hooked as a fan?

I first heard *I Want to Hold Your Hand* on the school bus in early 1964 and instantly fell for the music of the Beatles. The first album I bought (with a lot of help from my mom) was *Meet The Beatles!* I first saw the Beatles on *The Ed Sullivan Show.*

As you followed the Beatles, you would keep in constant touch with your record store awaiting new releases. Will you please tell us about that?

By 1968, I would learn of upcoming Beatles releases about a week in advance. I would call the record store daily until the record came in. I must have drove the store manager of Studio A Records crazy!!!

Tell us about how you came to learn of the Paul is Dead rumors, and how did you react to the news?

I first heard about the rumors on WTIX in New Orleans. I felt it was a false rumor and told many girls in my high school class not to worry.

As you are a repository of information, please give us an overview of your understanding of these rumors, will you?

It would take me way too long to properly give my understanding of the Paul is Dead rumors. I cover the Paul is Dead story in my book *The Beatles Get Back to Abbey Road* in two chapters, one that I wrote and one written by Frank Daniels. The chapters explain how the rumor got started and why it spread so fast in a time when there was no Internet.

Do you suspect that the Lads were having a 'lark', or what was at work behind all of this?

I truly believe that this was not a plot or joke by the Beatles. It was just a bunch of images, sounds and false statements that were called 'clues' to support the theory that Paul was dead, when in fact he wasn't. As the rumors started on college campuses, it was a case of some students with too much time on their hands and probably too much pot.

Did you ever play your records backwards?

I played and taped *Revolution No. 9* backwards in its entirety. Hearing what sounds like "Turn me on dead man" was very creepy then, and still is!!!

By Abbey Road, *the 'clues' were abundant. What do you make of all that?*

Nothing intentional on the Beatles' part. Just fun to spot images and try to tie in into this great conspiracy that Paul is dead.

Did you spot any clues that less keen eyes may have missed?

On *Yesterday And Today*, if you turn the LP front cover sideways, it looks like Paul is lying in a coffin (in this case a steamer trunk) with the lid being closed by Ringo, who is supposedly dressed as an undertaker of the cover of *Abbey Road*. If you turn the front cover to *Revolver* sideways, it looks like Paul is lying face up (as he would be if buried in a coffin).

So, is Paul still with us? Where do you cast your vote?

The man who wrote and sang lead on *All My Loving* is the same man who wrote and sang lead on *Hey Jude*. 'Nuff Said!!!

Jon Provost

Jon Provost began his acting career at age two, in the film *So Big*. As a busy child actor, he went on to appear onscreen with huge names like Grace Kelly, Bing Crosby, Natalie Wood, Rod Steiger, Robert Redford, and Clint Eastwood. He is probably best remembered for his role as Timmy in the iconic *Lassie* television series.

Please tell us about yourself, and any projects that you are working on, will you?

Jon keeps busy volunteering at children's hospitals, animal shelters, and has served on the Board of Directors for Canine Companions for Independence, an organization that provides extraordinary service dogs to the handicapped, for more than twenty years. Jon has received numerous awards, among them The Motion Picture Council's award for Outstanding Contribution as a Humanitarian for his dedication to helping the physically challenged, the Allen Ludden Humanitarian Award presented by Betty White, and the Lifetime Achievement Award from the Youth in Film Association.

When did you first become aware of the Beatles, and how long did it take for you to become a fan?

The first time I heard them and *I Want to Hold Your Hand* I wasn't impressed, I actually thought this song was a little lame. But then I got it especially the way the girls were reacting to them. Then of course I became a big fan like everyone else and I was lucky enough to see them twice in concert. First at Dodger Stadium then at the Hollywood Bowl in 1966. Of course I've seen Ringo and Paul on tour for many years.

Do you have a favorite Beatle, and why did they appeal to you?

My favorite Beatle was Ringo because he was the "Silly" one and I always liked drummers although I never played the drums.

What was Lassie's favorite Beatle album, and why?

Let's see, that would be *Let it Be* because of the song *The Long and Winding Road*, Lassie like to take long walks.

Can you tell us what it was like working with Bing Crosby, Grace Kelly, Anita Ekberg, and an uncredited Clint Eastwood?

Well I don't remember my first two movies, I was too young so I don't remember working with Bing or Grace; now I do remember working with Anita Ekberg. As you know she was a Swedish sex symbol and she loved holding me in her lap and I didn't mind a bit As a matter of fact, I remember some of the crew members offering me five dollars to trade places, LOL. I never did get to work with Clint on *Escapade in Japan*, he was in the states while I was in Japan and we never met.

When did you first hear about the Paul is Dead rumors, and what were your thoughts about that?

Well like everyone else, I believe in 1969. I never believed it because I knew there were always rumors about people in show business or the entertainment industry that were not true, just publicity. You know what they say, "all publicity is good" whether it's true or not.

Did you ever play your vinyl records backwards?

Yes like everyone else, the *White Album* I recall the most, never did hear anything, though. Donovan also convinced me to try *Mellow Yellow*, nothing there either LOL.

What 'clues' stand out to you on the record album covers?

Can't answer that one.

Some say the Beatles stopped touring because Paul had been replaced. Why do you think the Beatles stopped playing live?

I think they stopped touring because they could be more experimental in the studio, live concerts were just too limiting, too old school. I mean really, how could you play *Sgt. Pepper* live? *I Want to Hold Your Hand*, yes, *Magical Mystery Tour*, no way.

So, is Paul still with us? Where do you cast your vote?
    Yes, it's the real Paul today, he never left us.

Richard Syrett

Richard Syrett is a veteran radio personality, host of *The Conspiracy Show, Strange Planet,* and *The Richard Syrett Show.* He is also a regular guest host on *Coast to Coast AM.*

Please tell us about yourself, and your work.
    I've been in talk radio for most of my adult life, starting in the early 90s as a producer at Toronto radio station CFRB AM 1010. In 2000 I began hosting my own talk show about high strangeness, UFOs, conspiracies and the paranormal. In 2010, I created, wrote, and hosted a documentary style television program called *The Conspiracy Show,* which was sold in the international market. In 2013 I starred in a TV pilot for Discovery called *The United States of Paranoia,* which investigated alleged cases of electronic harassment and mind control. Starting in January 2014 I became a regular weekend guest-host on *Coast to Coast AM,* the most listened to late-night, talk-show in the world. I've just wrapped up a 13-year stint on Toronto Radio Station AM 740 Zoomer Radio as host of *Strange Planet.* These days I am focused on my daily afternoon-drive program, *The Richard Syrett Show,* on Toronto-area radio station News Talk SAUGA 960 AM. No UFOs, no ghost hunters, no conspiracies, just straight-up news, views and interviews. I continue to produce three episodes a week of my podcast Richard Syrett's Strange Planet. For more information on *The Richard Syrett Show* visit www.therichardsyrettshow.com. The podcast is available everywhere you get podcasts. You can subscribe to the premium platform for at https://strangeplanet. supportingcast.fm

When did you first see the Beatles, and how long did it take for you to be hooked and become a fan?

I have very early memories of seeing the Beatles perform their singles *Hey Jude* and *Revolution* on *The Smothers Brothers Comedy Hour*. This would have been in 1968, so I was nearly five. By this time, of course, the Beatles had stopped performing live, but they released what were, I suppose, what you'd call early iterations of music videos, which they'd filmed at Twickenham Studios in Great Britain. Those clips aired on British TV shows like *Top of the Pops* and journalist David Frost's program, *Frost on Sunday*. But the Beatles chose the Smothers Brothers program in the US because their song *Revolution* fit in with the Smothers Brothers reputation as being controversial and anti-establishment. A few years later, once I was allowed to operate the family portable Viking record player, I discovered my eldest sister's stash of 45s which included, *I Am the Walrus* and *Hey Bull Dog*. I remember thinking to myself, "what a strange and wonderful sound!" I also remember thinking, "I am the walrus? What on earth are these strange looking young men singing about?"

In the late 70s, during a high school class trip to Toronto and the legendary record shop, Sam the Record Man, I purchased the *Blue Album*, a double compilation and re-mastered release of the Beatles singles from 1967 to 1970 from EMI. My best friend at the time, Tom Balan, and I played that album almost every day after school for a year and a half.

The night John Lennon died, I was at Tom's and we had the *Monday Night Football* game on, but we had the sound turned down because we were listening to and singing along to that EMI Beatles record. We missed Howard Cosell's announcement that Lennon had been shot in the back outside his New York City apartment. "Rushed to Roosevelt hospital... dead on arrival." I remember walking home that night, singing *Strawberry Fields Forever,* dreaming of a Beatles reunion, oblivious to the horror that had transpired just an hour or so before.

Do you think that the major loss of JFK helped to propel the Beatles to the top of the charts, as people needed something to forget their troubles?

I know this is the conventional wisdom, and it's almost considered sacrilege to suggest otherwise, but I'm not entirely convinced this was the case. There's no doubt Americans were in need of some joyful diversion after their president was brutally murdered. And in the months following his death, there were countless diversions available to American consumers. Do we then attribute the popularity of all of these diversions to the slaying of a popular young president? No one to my knowledge is arguing that Bobby Vinton, who had eleven top 40 hits in the year following JFK's death, was successful because of the Kennedy assassination. Was a nation mourning Kennedy's death responsible for the success of popular TV shows like *The Beverly Hillbillies, Bonanza* and *The Dick Van Dyke Show?* I don't think so.

I suspect these four loveable, intelligent, funny songsmiths from England would have been wildly popular in America with or without the tragic events of November 22nd, 1963. We'll never know for sure, of course, but it's not as if the Fab Four were complete unknowns when they touched down at newly named John F. Kennedy Airport in February 1964. The lads had their first smash hit in America two months before they arrived. In December 1963, the band released *I Want to Hold Your Hand* in America and the single sold three-quarters of a million copies in just three days.

Their success could just as easily be explained by an interview they did with Mike Wallace for *The CBS Morning News*, which aired that very same fateful day of November 22nd. The interview was to be replayed that same night but was bumped for obvious reasons. While it is true the Beatles arrival in February 1964 marked the beginning of the British Invasion of blues infused rock and roll, nobody attributes the success of The Animals, The Rolling Stones, The Kinks, or The Zombies to Kennedy's death. Why is that? Maybe it's because these British musicians were just really talented.

The Sixties seems to have been a veritable hotbed for conspiracies of various types. Why were things so stirred up in that decade?

The tumultuousness of the 1960s can be explained, in part, by three important societal forces: the affluence of the post-Second World War period; secularization of the culture; and general boredom amongst the boomer generation. These factors all helped create a fertile ground and a receptive audience for the introduction of radical left-wing ideology on college campuses. And all of these forces, in turn, helped pave the way for the second wave feminist movement, the so-called sexual revolution, and the sex, drugs and rock and roll culture. The introduction of widespread LSD use into the culture before it was criminalized nationwide in the fall of 1966, and the creation of the psychedelic scene had a tremendous impact on the culture and on politics. The initial wave of the anti-Vietnam war movement, which began in earnest at the teach-ins at the University of Michigan on March 24, 1965, was, no doubt, comprised of certain influential individuals who began their activist careers after having their "doors of perception" blown off after their first encounter with lysergic acid diethylamide. The same can probably be said for those who began questioning the official narrative of the Kennedy assassination following the release of the Warren Commission Report in the fall of 1964. This is in no way meant to suggest that only people who were tripping on acid believed the Vietnam War was immoral or that Kennedy was the victim of a vast conspiracy. But we are learning that while LSD can mimic psychosis, it can also lead to what researchers call "cognitive looseness," characterized by highly enhanced mental flexibility. Perhaps this is what Aldous Huxley was referring to in 1954 when he published *The Doors of Perception* in which he chronicled his psychedelic experience under the influence of mescaline.

There is a widely accepted conspiracy theory that Timothy Leary's Harvard experiments with LSD, and later the Acid Test parties put on by Ken Kesey and his Merry Pranksters, with musical accompaniment provided by the Grateful Dead, were all funded and promoted by the CIA. The theory goes that the CIA and the military-industrial complex believed that the introduction of LSD into the culture by the CIA could be used to pacify the population and thus prevent wide-spread opposition to the Vietnam War and the public execution of a president. Ironically, the introduction of LSD into the culture had precisely the opposite effect.

Do you recall when you first heard the rumors that Paul may have shed his mortal coil, and been replaced by a double?

Around the same time (Fall of 1979) I purchased the EMI collection of the Beatles 1967-1970 at Sam the Record Man in Toronto, and was playing it non-stop, a neighbor, and my older brother's best friend, tried to tell me about the Paul is Dead conspiracy. I didn't take much of what he told me seriously, because he was a notorious prankster who was always looking for ways to take the mickey out of me. I assumed this was just another one of his pranks. Several years later I was at The Toronto Old Book and Paper Show and one of the vendors had a booth chalk-o-block full of Beatles collectibles, including a copy of the November 1969 *Life* magazine issue with Paul and Linda on the front cover, titled 'Paul is Still with Us.' He wouldn't allow me to take the magazine out of its plastic sleeve to read for myself. Instead he took the time to explain to me how *Life*'s London correspondent waded through a Scotland bog and found Paul and Linda at their secluded Scotland farm. Paul had been pretty quiet since the breakup of The Beatles. The correspondent asked Paul about the various "death clues," which Paul dismissed as "bloody stupid." That really piqued my curiosity and so I immediately followed that up with a little reading of my own and that's when I read about Detroit DJ Russ Gibb on WKNR-FRM taking a call from a listener in October 1969 who was eager to discuss rumors of McCartney's death which were swirling around. Roby Young at WABC in New York went to air with the story around the same time, October '69. Young apparently heard the rumor from a group of college kids attending Indiana University

Bloomington. After Young made the announcement on air several national newspapers picked up on the story and Young was fired.

What 'clues' stand out to you from the Beatle album covers in regards to Paul, and all of that business?

My late friend, R. Gary Patterson, rock historian and author of *The Walrus was Paul* showed me how to take the straight edge of a mirror and line it up across the middle of the words, 'LONELY HEARTS' written across the centre of the bass drum on the cover of *Sgt. Pepper's*. When you do that you see "1ONEIX HE (diamond shape) DIE." The 1ONEIX could suggest the eleventh month November (1 and One is eleven) and IX is the ninth day. This corresponds to the date of McCartney's supposed death, November 9th, 1966. The diamond shape appears to point directly at Paul's image on the album cover. Putting it all together, here's what you get: November 9th He (diamond pointing at Paul) die. The only problem is that in Great Britain they write dates day/month/year, rather than month/day/year like we do in North America. That would make the date of Paul's death September 11th instead of November 9th. So another explanation is that I ONE IX could mean, "I, one of four is gone…and then HE DIE points to Paul.

Some say that the Beatles stopped touring because Paul was replaced. Why do you think that the Beatles stopped touring?

Sorry Beatles conspiracy fans, but the boring prosaic explanation is The Beatles simply got fed up with not being able to hear themselves play over the colossal noise and incessant screaming from the crowds. It must have been incredibly frustrating for the Beatles as musicians and songsmiths to have played under those conditions. I've heard fans who attended Beatles concerts describe the sound as a sonic mess. Demand to see them live was so huge that promoters had to scramble and find the biggest venues available, which in most cities meant the sports stadium. But in the mid-60s, the technology to amplify the sound properly to fill such a venue simply didn't exist. The Beatles had only their tiny little amps and the sound was then fed through the stadium PA system. The sound must have been terribly distorted. I imagine I would have been incredibly disappointed if I had the chance to have seen them live.

Did you ever play any of your vinyl records backwards?

I tried a few times and ruined the needle. So, don't do that, kids!

What 'clues' from the songs stand out most to you?

Sgt. Pepper's was the first album in history to include the lyrics printed out. On the back of the album cover we see George Harrison. He's pointing to a line in the song, *She's Leaving Home.* The line is Wednesday morning at five o'clock as the day begins. This was supposedly the day and time of Paul's fatal car wreck.

So, is Paul still with us? Where do you cast your vote?

I am about ninety-nine percent sure that Sir Paul McCartney is still very much with us. I say this with some degree of certainty knowing how a musician and lyricist of the caliber of a Paul McCartney comes around once in a lifetime. If he had perished in a fiery car crash on the M-1 on November 9th 1966, how, one is left to explain, did the orchestrators of this hoax manage to find another uber-talented, left-handed bass player that looked enough like Paul, even with plastic surgery, to fool the world? If that really is William Campbell or William Sheppard and not Paul McCartney still out there touring, recording and thrilling audiences into his eighties, he is arguably more talented than the original Paul who, supposedly perished in the driver's seat of his Austin Healey.

Carol Shaw

Carol Shaw is an author, who notably served as show business icon Bob Hope's secretary.

Please tell the readers about yourself, and about your work.

I am the proud author of *Bob Hope's Bungalow: Tales from the Typing Trenches* which has just been published by BearManor Media and available for sale. You can also find my book at Amazon.com. My book is a light-hearted, irreverent look at my time in 1983 and 1984 when I worked for the legendary funnyman Bob Hope. It chronicles my time at Mr. Hope's Toluca Lake residence with Bob, his zany writers, long-suffering, hilarious staff, and many celebrity friends. I was hired as Secretary #2 and worked in The Bungalow which is the small building/cottage adjacent to Bob's Mansion. No one gets past The Bungalow without the guard opening the large wooden gate separating the luxurious Mansion from the office staff diligently working inside The Bungalow.

When did you first become aware of the Beatles, and how long before you were hooked?

It was in late 1961 or early 1962 when my British grandmother mailed me pictures of the latest pop music band that was taking over England called The Beatles. They were huge! I had been aware of them because of the teen magazines at the local drug stores in Winnipeg, Canada heralding the impending British Invasion. I was over the moon to get these treasured newspaper clippings and magazine pictures from England and was "hooked" immediately on those four cute, mop-topped lads from Liverpool! *I Want to Hold Your Hand* was their first song, and I welcomed the Invasion!

Which one of the Beatles was your favorite and why do they appeal to you?

My absolute favorite was Paul McCartney because he was the smartest and the cutest of all of them. Plus, he smiled a lot and had the ability to shake his hair. They all shook their mop-top hair, but Paul stood out. John seemed much older and darker. George had a unibrow. Ringo was second on the adorableness scale. The songs that The Beatles sang were so innocent and had a beat. Perfect for any teenybopper in those days.

Tell us the story behind your Beatles autographed photo?

I was one of those latch-key kids where the parents were both working all day. I was all alone in the house. When I got home from school, I was like any other kid and was bored out of my gourd. (Remember, there were no cell phones, no Internet, and no adult supervision!) This one day I invited two of my girlfriends over to my house. We did the usual girl things, looking at teen magazines, putting on my mother's make-up, walking around like we were models on the catwalk. I showed them my treasure trove of Beatles' photos and we were all giggling at mooning over the cute Beatles. Then I came up with the bright idea of talking to them. I had seen my mother dial zero on the phone before and speak to an Operator who would connect the Transatlantic call to England so my mum could speak to my British grandmother in Oxford. It looked so easy!

I got the long-distance Operator on the phone and asked for Paul McCartney in Liverpool, England. Oddly enough, the Operator was glad to do it. (I think she was also a fan of the Beatles.) That call just rang and rang. The Operator asked if I wanted to dial another number. Of course, I did! I asked that she dial Jane Asher's home. (She was the actress girlfriend of Paul at the time.) The Operator connected the call and someone at Jane's house did answer the phone. Unfortunately, Jane was not in. By this time my young friends were offering up other suggestions like, call Maureen Cox at the Liverpool beauty salon (Ringo's girlfriend at the time). Oh, we had the dirt of which girlfriend belonged to which Beatle, and just went down the list. The Operator couldn't get Maureen on the phone, either. In fact, the Operator suggested we call the EMI Recording Studios in London (later Abbey Road Studios) where the Beatles practiced. Long story short, a man with a Cockney accent answered the phone. I asked for Paul. He wasn't around at the moment said the man. Why did I want to talk to Paul he asked. My response was that I was a fan from Canada and just wanted to talk to the Beatles! The man, who I later learned was Malcolm, said he was their roadie and did I want a picture of the Beatles instead. What kid would say no to that? I gave him my address in Winnipeg. Malcolm said he'd mail the picture out later that day. I hung up and then all three of us screamed in unison because I had spoken to Malcolm at the Beatles' studio! It was exciting to say the least.

It was several months later when the big envelope from Britain arrived early on a Saturday morning at exactly the same day as the Canadian phone bill. When my mum opened the bill, she went ballistic! It was way over $50 and she was furious! Steam was coming out of her ears. I don't think I had seen my mother so angry! The British don't fool around when they are upset. I was dragged out of bed by my arm to a whole lot of yelling and shaking from my mother! I felt like a rag doll. I told dear old mum that I had called England looking for the Beatles. That excuse did not go over very well. Yes, I got a "hiding" (aka beating) by my mum for doing a very bad thing and especially by not telling her about it, not to mention the cost of calling all over England! Sure, it wasn't like I had killed anybody, but my mum made me feel very guilty. To this day, I'm really scared of calling overseas for any reason. I still have family in Oxford, England but there is no way, I'd ever call them!

The Beatles had a song called Hey Bulldog. *We hear rumors that Bob Hope had some special dogs. Do tell about them, will you?*

Back in 1983 and 1984 I had worked for Bob Hope at his Toluca Lake home. Bob's special dogs were Shadow and Snowjob. Shadow was a black Labrador and Snowjob was the white one. There were the "family pets" but also the guard dogs at Mr. Hope's Toluca Lake residence. They were trained to keep out strangers from entering the Hope compound and were very good at it. The dogs had the run of the place and always came into The Bungalow where the office staff worked. Many a writer who had turned their backs on the dogs was "gifted" with a nip in the butt which drew blood. I had heard the stories of the biting dogs before but didn't realize how much mayhem could arise.

Apparently, one of the secretaries before me had gone on vacation. She loved those dogs and always played with them outside. When she came back from vacation, she did her usual thing and went outside to pet the dogs. No one thought anything of it until screams were heard. The poor secretary came running back into The Bungalow with both dogs chasing her. She was hysterical! The dogs had attacked her, biting her breast and hand so badly she had to be rushed to the hospital! After the surgery, the secretary found she couldn't use her hand very well due to the dog bites. She asked Bob to pay her hospital bills, but he dug in his heels. There wasn't any insurance for secretaries (like every office has today). No, the eighties were a different era. In the end, the poor secretary threatened to sue Bob for her injuries. He paid, but he wasn't a happy camper about letting go of his money. The happy ending was that the secretary retired to Hawaii and opened a gift shop.

Another instance was when the first female staff writer hired by Bob, Martha Bolton, got chomped on by one of the dogs. I saw this for myself! Martha and I were just walking down the hall toward the front door when the dog sniffed Martha's foot. She didn't react because all she was doing was walking with me. It happened so fast. The dog was next to me, then walked around to Martha's side and suddenly bit into her foot. For a moment she didn't even realize what had happened. She stopped and looked down at her foot, which now had blood on it, and said "I think the dog just bit me." Martha must have been in shock, but then the pain started. Her husband was outside in the car, and they immediately drove over to the local hospital where she was treated. This time, Bob Hope footed the bill and paid for everything without question.

Did you ever play your records backwards looking for clues?
I tried, but I was clueless!

The record covers had some clues, and they supposedly were telling us that Paul had shed his mortal coil. Did any album cover clues stick out to you?

No, I was not convinced of it at all. I think the clues were just manufactured by advertising executives in order to sell more Beatles albums. Congratulations, it worked!

Would you please tell us the anecdote describing the events of Dolores Hope going to see the Pope? What was Bob Doing at the time?

Since Dolores Hope (nee DeFina) and her sister were staunch Catholics, they were obsessed with getting blessed by the Pope. They finally got a meeting with his Excellency and flew to Italy. Bob stayed behind at their Toluca Lake residence in California due to his constant work schedule. Since he was on his own, there was no chance Bob would get caught trying to smuggle in an old "lady friend." All he had to do was drive in and get past the guard at the gate without arising suspicion! The lady was usually hidden from the guard. Everyone knew what was going on but didn't say a word. What could you say? It was just Bob being Bob!

The Beatles had a nifty little number called Drive My Car. *Would you please tell us about Bob Hope's driving practices in Toluca Lake?*

Bob usually was driven around Toluca Lake by his handyman, Armando. But it was always a fight to see who'd get behind the wheel. Bob loved to drive, but he was notorious for his bad driving. It wasn't his fault! He had a progressive eye disease in later years which made seeing things difficult, to say the least. Thank God Armando did most of the driving. On the occasions that he didn't, Bob took the wheel and they were off to the races as the car crept over the middle line in the road or scraped a car or two parked along the side. As all of this was happening, Armando gripped his rosary and prayed aloud in Spanish to the Blessed Virgin Mary for them to get to their destination in one piece! The Teluca Lake cops who were out on patrol always give Bob Hope a wide berth. None of them wanted to be the cop on the force to arrest the legendary Bob Hope!

So, is Paul still with us? Where do you cast your vote?

I believe Paul McCartney is still alive and making music. He's one of the few people whose career has never died and he's having a ball! He kind of reminds me of the late Bob Hope. The great ones never go away. They live on in our memories. Thanks for the Memory!

Gavin Pring

Gavin Pring is an internationally renowned musician best known for touring in a popular Beatles tribute band.

Please tell us about yourself and your band, and what's new, will you?

My name's Gavin Pring and I perform in an internationally touring Beatles tribute band show called "The Fab Four"... On the horizon we're looking forward to headlining Liverpool *Beatleweek*, like we have done a few times and catching up with family and friends while I'm over there...

You hail from Liverpool, just like the Lads. How does Liverpool look upon their favorite sons, and what was it like growing up there?

Yes, I'm a true native Liverpudlian, or as the locals would say, a scouser, and I think being born there and seeing the poverty and the success that the city has had to endure, may give me an inside perspective on what the Beatles themselves may have experienced from their time here...

For a little while (in the 80's for sure), I felt people didn't admit to being "Beatle fans" and I reckon this is due, in part, to the rising stars and bands that were trying to get out of the shadow of the

Beatles... Liverpool was not only home to a "successful band" but arguably the best band in the history of the world! New bands tried to express themselves without leaning directly on the Beatles, groups like Frankie goes to Hollywood and Echo and the Bunnymen but found themselves being "compared" to the Beatles because of their shared origin... It's hard enough to make a living in a band, let alone being compared to the best band ever!

However, to answer the question, I do believe that those bands, and most people in Liverpool, even though they couldn't admit it the time, did (and still do), share a love and fascination with the Beatles... Not only their music, but the stamp that they proudly put on the world! Even though they found superstardom, they still sang about people and locations familiar to all scousers, *Eleanor Rigby* and *Penny Lane* for example...

To quote an interview with Ringo (which I may not do verbatim). Ringo was asked "Do you ever visit Liverpool?" To which he responded "Not really"...

"What about Paul?"

"Paul? Oh Paul never left"...

This answer is funny to me because it illustrates the 2 mindsets, 1, leave and never come back and 2, leave but never really leave... Obviously, they left, but Liverpool never forgot them, except in the 80's...

Aside from mastering the guitar, you also have played the sitar at shows. What is it like playing that instrument, compared to a guitar?

Playing guitar is like playing golf, you never really feel you've mastered it because there's always so much more to learn; however, comparing guitar to the sitar? LOL, I've only really ever played the solo to *Within You Without You*, believe me, even those few licks were difficult, you have to sit a certain way, you have to hold it a certain way, you have this thing clamped to your index finger (I think it's called a misrab) and you pluck the main string towards you... so, it's nothing like playing a guitar...I think a couple of centuries ago, an old Indian guy found a tree that had been wrapped up in fallen power lines during a storm and said "I'm gonna play that!!" Even though the instrument itself is difficult, the music from it is beautiful, it has definitely given me a greater appreciation of Eastern music and especially for the sitar players...

When did you first become aware of the Beatles, and how long was it before you became a fan?

I first became aware of the Beatles when I was born and opened my eyes!! Tbh, I can't remember a time when the Beatles weren't around; however, I do remember the first album that I really listened to and really became a fan...A girl in school (that I fancied) loved the Beatles and I asked her what her favourite album was and she said the *White Album* so that night with a Walkman in hand, fully-charged batteries and headphones in place I loaded the *White Album* cassette in and started to listen to it, in the dark...The Walkman had an auto-return feature, which meant, when it reached the end of side 1 it would just automatically start the beginning of side 2 and, again it would return to side 1 and so on...So, that night, I never went to sleep, I saw the sun rise and ran the batteries dry but I was hooked, I'd been reborn a completely, true, converted Beatles fan...

Asking your favorite Beatle would likely find George as the answer for obvious reasons. Instead, will you please tell us who your second favorite Beatle is?

George actually isn't my favourite Beatle; he did produce my favourite Beatle songs and I think he was the coolest Beatle but I've always been a Lennon fan...I have a painting of John in my living room which my wife, after winning a jackpot on a $2.00 machine in Vegas bought for me...I had been looking at this awesome painting of John that was in this gallery in the Miracle Mile shops at the Planet Hollywood, we had a show there for a couple of years and every day I would look at it just before I had to get ready for the show...One day, we finished a performance and I went backstage and the art-piece was in my dressing room, I couldn't believe it...

Anyway, I digress, John seemed to be the straight-shooter to me, his contributions to the Beatles songs and collaborations with Paul always had a directness that scousers (And East Coast Americans) seem to respect...Paul would sing "Try to see it my way! Only time will tell if I am right or I am wrong" while John would retort "Life is very short, and there's no time for fussing and fighting my friend"... Those kind of direct, no bullshit lyrics just kinda struck a chord with me, and obviously lots of other people...We love all the Beatles but John's my favourite ...

When did you first hear that Paul McCartney was rumored to have been replaced by a double? What did you make of that?

Well, I was never around when the rumor originally came out, I was retroactively researching them and their music, but when I read that there was a big conspiracy about it I thought, well, if it was true, I'd take the 2nd Paul any day...He wrote *The Long and Winding Road* and *Maybe I'm Amazed* and *Jet* and *Let it Be* etc, etc. I mean, what are the chances that the REAL Paul died and then the record company or the band got a guy who looked exactly the same, sang the same and was left-handed and then wrote better tunes?? I've been in the Beatle impersonator business for a long time, we've been looking for Paul's for years, but they, magically found a guy, with all those coincidental, natural abilities and, was the exact same age?? Come on! Like most conspiracy theories, very, very entertaining and usually, very, very false!

Which clues about the Paul rumors were most interesting to you from the album covers?

I suppose the most interesting album cover clue is the role representation on the *Abbey Road* album, I like the idea that the Beatles were so wracked with guilt about hiring William Campbell that they left their fans clues not only through visual means but by leaving audio clues in their songs that required their fans to rotate the albums "backwards" to be revealed...Again, going back to the question, the idea that as the lads crossed Abbey Road, that John represented the heavenly spirit (which I'm sure John would've gotten a kick out of) while Paul is barefoot, obviously dead, Ringo the undertaker and George the denim-wearing gravedigger... just magic!! Like John said "You can make anything fit, man!"

Did you ever play your records backwards?
     Nope.

Is it true that during your Vegas residency with the Fab Four, that a very much alive Elvis inquired if Paul was replaced back in the day?
     As we were getting ready one day for our show in Las Vegas a very much alive Elvis asked us if he could play out with our Paul. With us not being able to control our Paul and his life decisions we had no choice but to accept the unusual request...As we watched the 2 new friends playing catch, bobbing for apples and trying to find each other during a grueling session of Hide & Seek, we noticed that, as the sun receded behind the horizon, and as the light faded, and as, we stood there, squinting our already squinty eyes, that yes, almost inexplicably, the 2 historical megastars, were, in fact, just 2 impersonators enjoying a weird and wonderful day together...

What do you make of Paul's solo career, which would have featured a double if the rumors are true?
     (Don't really have an answer for this one; I'm more familiar with John and George's solo work than Paul's unfortunately).

Some say that the Beatles stopped touring because Paul was replaced. Why do you think that the Beatles stopped touring?
     I believe the Beatles stopped touring for a few reasons, maybe because of the limited volume at their live concerts that they weren't having as much fun "on stage" because they couldn't hear themselves,

or each other...The touring life is difficult, not much rest, constantly changing time zones, even Ringo thought he was in New York when he was in Washington DC and obviously he laughed about it, but it is difficult to find a balance being away that much you know...Being tired goes directly against creating new songs, I think they didn't want to be performing monkeys for the rest of their lives so they wanted to get back to producing new material...Technology had changed which allowed better recording techniques...And, they had young kids, maybe the idea of going to the same place, day in, day out gave them a better chance of having a semi-normal life.. Who knows, probably all of those reasons played a part...

So, is Paul still with us? Where do you cast your vote?

I think you know where my vote is cast on the "Is Paul really dead?" question...It's a definitive "No", however, rumour has it that Ringo, and, this is weird, was actually undercover in the late eighties as the WWF's "The Undertaker" in which he wore a mask and had stilts on, to give him a bit of extra height. Obviously, as the last surviving Beatle he wanted to re-affirm to his true fans that he still felt bad about hiding the truth and that he was, indeed, the undertaker... Again "You can make anything fit, man!"

And in the End

- It's the most stupid rumor I've ever heard

John Lennon, 1969

As can be seen by most of the interviews in this book, there is widespread skepticism about the "Paul is Dead" legend. Bob Wilson and I both agree with almost everyone else who was questioned by us. Paul McCartney didn't die in 1966. He remains alive and well. But still, thereare enough intriguing tidbits to keep people wondering.

I watched a video online that featured clips of the other Beatles, George Harrison's wife, comedian Dana Carvey, and others all seeming to greet McCartney as "Bill," "Billy," or "William." This would, of course, refer to the William Campbell, aka Billy Shears, that is at the heart of the theory. Were they all just having fun with a ridiculous rumor? Had they all just adopted it as an inside joke? Another video analyzes several pictures of a bare-chested McCartney, focusing on a mole that is clearly visible near his right nipple in early years, but gone in later photos.

McCartney's volatile ex-wife Heather Mills made some provocative comments that have been interpreted to refer to the "Paul is Dead" legend. In a November 1, 2007 interview with Billy Bush on Access Hollywood, Mills stated, "Something so awful happened. Someone I'd loved for a long time I found out had betrayed me immensely. And I don't mean infidelity or anything like that. Like, beyond belief. People don't want to know what the truth is because they could never ever handle it. They would be too devastated." She then spoke directly to McCartney, saying, "You know why I've left you. Protect me and I will say nothing." In another interview, with Fiona Phillips on the British television show GMTV, Mills reiterated, "I have protected my husband. I know everything, and I know the truth." She then warned that, "I have a box of evidence that is going to a certain person should anything happen to me. So if you top me off, it's still gonna go to that certain person, and the truth will come out. There is such a fear from a certain party of the truth coming out."

Even assuming the Beatles were able to find a McCartney-lookalike, who could sing, play music, and write great songs as well as (or better) than the original Paul, there is the reality of what happened to the band in the years after 1966, the year of the alleged accident. As was alluded to in the Introduction, Paul McCartney took over. He became the undeniable leader of the Beatles, a position John Lennon had held during the early years. The later Beatles albums are dominated by McCartney's work, including Sgt. Pepper and Abbey Road. If the theory is correct, this would mean that Billy Shears proved to be even more prolific than the real Paul McCartney, and perhaps more importantly, that John Lennon was willing to abdicate his leadership to a mere replacement. One would think that an artist talented enough to write such iconic tunes would have already been front and center of his own band.

John Lennon expounded on the subject, in an angry rant on a Detroit radio station: "It sounds like the same guy who blew up my Christ remark. I don't know what Beatles records sound like backwards, I never play them backwards. They said I was wearing a white religious suit. I mean, did Humphrey Bogart wear a white religious suit? All I've got is a nice Humphrey Bogart suit." Lennon declared. In 1974, McCartney joked, "Someone from the office rang me up and said: 'Look, Paul, you're dead.' And I said, 'Oh, I don't agree with that.'" McCartney continued, "They said: 'Look, what are you going to do about it? It's a big thing breaking in America. You're dead.' And so I said, leave it, just let them say it. It'll probably be the best publicity we've ever had, and I won't have to do a thing except stay alive. So I managed to stay alive through it." As Lennon admitted, it would have been a "great plug" for their work.

Bob and I each feel strongly that the clues on the albums and in lyrics heard both forwards and backwards, cannot be dismissed as coincidence. Simply put, we believe that the Beatles created the "Paul is Dead" myth as a public relations ploy. That doesn't detract from their incomparable record of creating brilliant, timeless music. The Beatles, like Dickens and Shakespeare, are British artists who will probably be remembered hundreds of years from now. This book was produced by a couple of huge fans, and was a genuine labor of love.

Printed in Great Britain
by Amazon

32180879R00116